ESSENTIAL

ENGLISH COUNTRY

STYLE

ESSENTIAL
ENGLISH COUNTRY
STYLE

YVONNE REES

WARD LOCK

A WARD LOCK BOOK

First published in the UK 1995
by Ward Lock
Wellington House
125 Strand
LONDON
WC2R 0BB

A Cassell Imprint

Distributed in the United States
by Sterling Publishing Co., Inc,
387 Park Avenue South, New York,
NY 10016-8810

Distributed in Australia
by Capricorn Link (Australia) Pty Ltd
2/13 Carrington Road, Castle Hill
NSW 2154

A British Library Cataloguing in
Publication Data block for this book
may be obtained from the British
Library

ISBN 0-7063-7415-0

Designed by Nick Clark
Illustrations by Jane Hughes
Printed and bound in Spain

CONTENTS

$\mathcal{I}$NTRODUCTION

IF YOU COULD ONLY BLEND AND BOTTLE the essence of what we imagine to be the typical English country house or cottage, the dominant 'notes' would surely be those of sweet woodsmoke, a rose and lavender-based pot pourri and heady beeswax polish – perhaps with undertones of Earl Grey, newly-mown grass and damp spaniel. Now close your eyes and conjure up the sound of birdsong in a garden refreshed by a recent shower of rain; the crackle of logs on an open fire; bees buzzing and the distant sound of church bells pealing. And is there honey still for tea? There certainly is – in addition to floral chintz fabrics and heavy brocades, low oak beams and comfy sofas, a Rayburn and a huge pine table groaning with home-made goodies in the kitchen.

Quintessential English country style is rooted in the past. It looks like a home that has developed gradually over the centuries, each generation adding their own favourite features and furnishings: it is a multi-layered look rich in detail that would fascinate an interiors archaeologist. Comfortable, maybe even a little shabby if you examine it closely, this is definitely a style that benefits from looking a little worn if it is to be successful. That familiar blend of flowery fabrics, interesting rustic textures, well-polished antique woods, and maybe even a touch of something oriental, would never work if it was too slickly co-ordinated. The trick is to combine furniture and furnishings in a more subtle way, relying on colour, texture or their natural origins to link them together. A period property bristling with character features obviously goes a long way towards setting the scene: an inglenook fireplace, a low ceiling with exposed beams, flagstones on the floor, mullion windows – these are all part of the charm and make the perfect background for faded fabrics and traditional country furniture. However, an ancient English manor house or thatched cottage with roses around the door is not essential: that country atmosphere can be introduced into any home – even an urban one – with the right approach to decorating and furnishing.

Nor do you have to wait a couple of generations to achieve that 'layered' lived-in look; with an eye for the right combination of effects and a few crafty short-cuts, it can be created almost instantly – and on a budget too. Buying second-hand is ideal and need not mean investing in expensive antiques or costly reproductions. Imagine the effect of a few mismatched chairs around an old

As delightful as an English country garden: comfortable furniture and floral themes conspire to create an irresistibly relaxing atmosphere in the country home.

stripped pine table – they can always be painted or stained the same colour if you want to give the impression that they are part of a set. How much more authentic and homely they will look than, say, a glossy and rather-too-perfect reproduction country-style dining suite; it is an option that is available at a fraction of the cost too. Although you will find the recent passion for country style has spawned a plethora of suitable fabrics, furniture and accessories, even a revival in old decorative techniques, such as stencilling and mixing your own paints, reproducing the knocks and dints of time certainly remains more important than faking shapes and patterns when aspiring to create what we fondly imagine is the rural English idyll. If you cannot buy second-hand, new fabrics can be prematurely aged and faded using bleaching agents; modern net curtains might lose their almost fluorescent whiteness with a good soaking in cold tea; a few carefully chosen pieces of new furniture can be successfully mixed with junk-shop or sale-room bargains or disguised beneath rugs, cloths, shawls and throws. You can let your personality and preferences dominate to create a home full of character and interest rather than following the dictates of a certain manufactured 'look'.

Country style is relaxed, often packed with detail – even to the extent of looking rather cluttered. Even the grander interiors do not really stand on ceremony, relying on old-fashioned quality and comfort rather than ostentatious effects and fashion statements. The owner of one rather splendid ancient manor house in England, whose home is open to the public, came up with the ingenious idea of pushing two or three single beds together and constructing a home-made canopy above to create a rather grand looking large bed. It is handy for guests too, she says, as you simply pull the beds apart when required. You will soon develop an eye yourself for what might look good together and come up with novel ideas on how existing items can be used to generate the right kind of atmosphere.

As you start arranging your own possessions accordingly, or buying things that catch your eye in the shops, you will often find interesting collections emerging that can be suitably displayed:

china plates or ornaments, paper weights, clay pipes, or even a selection of old straw hats. Some items can be hung on the walls – the perfect way to decorate an uneven or less than perfect surface – or, alternatively, arrange themed items on that classic piece of country furniture, the dresser.

There are really two kinds of English country home interior: the comfy cluttered look with its massed florals, sagging or slightly crooked furniture and a wealth of possessions arranged on every available surface; and the more spartan approach where everything is pared down to a minimum – stripped and scrubbed wood or stone, simple furniture, plain ginghams and no frills or fripperies. Everything on view will be functional, from the plain pewter candlestick to the blue and white striped cups and plates on the dresser. Invariably, a country home will combine both these styles depending on which room is being furnished: the living room might be as cosy as the snug in the village pub, the hallway or kitchen that has to take the constant traffic of muddy boots might be more simply furnished with plain flags on the floor and stripped pine furniture. The self-indulgent main bedroom could boast a four-poster or half-tester bed, while the spare bedroom might be almost monastic with its plain whitewashed walls and simple bed relieved only by a richly coloured patchwork quilt.

The size of your rooms and the general style and period of your house will determine to a large extent whether you will be looking to create a comfortable cottage atmosphere or the rather grander style of England's country houses. The latter is only really a scaled-up version of the classic cottage look: the rugs may be plusher, the window pelmets deeper, the florals larger, and the elm or pine replaced by polished oak or mahogany, but the aim is still that of achieving a relaxed yet practical home environment, in harmony with the natural surroundings immediately beyond the front door.

So how can that look be achieved successfully? Well, firstly this book will provide you with both inspiration and practical advice. Browse through its pages and as you move from room to

room, you will pick up plenty of great ideas that can be applied or adapted to your own home. Each room section also has a range of exciting yet easy-to-follow projects that you may like to tackle yourself to add that special personal touch to your country-style decorations and furnishings. These are suitable for any level of skill and you may surprise yourself at how creative you can be. Do not be afraid to modify or expand these project ideas to suit your own plans. If you find you are really taken with a certain technique and would like to explore its possibilities further, there are more specialist books available or even courses run to help develop your skills in this area. You could also gain additional inspiration by making visits to museums, particularly those specializing in English rural life, and to stately homes; look carefully at the elements that make up the total look and study how they are put together so that you can apply them in a similar way at home. Unless you are a fanatical traditionalist, historical detail is not important and it does not matter if the raw materials are different. It is the addition of a tablecloth, the style of curtains or the juxtaposition of a few ornaments that can so often capture a certain atmosphere successfully.

You might also find it helpful to browse around your local junk shops or antique sale-rooms to see what is available within your budget; start collecting brochures, catalogues, swatches and samples of paint colours, fabrics and flooring so that you can experiment with putting different colours and patterns together to create the right kind of look. Most important, go home and take a long appraising look at your existing furnishings and possessions. You may find new ways of putting them together or even changing their appearance altogether by stripping, staining, dyeing, repainting, recovering or simply giving a new lease of life with a change of handles, a decorative trim or casual cover-ups like rugs and shawls. This is the beauty of English country style – the look is totally individual and adaptable, relying more on your own flair and character than on any hard and fast decorative rules, and it need not cost a fortune to create.

Opposite: The mellow warmth of polished wood is complemented by the rougher rustic features of exposed brick and a quarry tile floor.

CHAPTER ONE

ESSENTIAL ELEMENTS OF STYLE

AT FIRST SIGHT, THE TYPICAL ENGLISH country interior may not look particularly well planned; nor do its decor and furnishings appear meticulously balanced and overtly co-ordinated like many of the slicker, more modern urban decorative schemes we are used to. Yet if you make a closer study, you will detect a subtle harmony, a sense of things looking good together and an underlying balance of colours and textures. Importantly, the raw materials used in putting a room together in a country home – the flooring, furnishings and furniture – need to be practical as well as good looking. They must be tough to take hard wear and be easy to clean. Often they will be natural materials, a logical link with the garden and countryside outside – stone, brick, dried grasses, stripped timber, cotton, wool, silk – creating a wonderful contrast of textures.

Colours also take their lead from nature: earthy russets, deep leafy greens, the deep, dark blue of a summer sky at midnight; or watery pastels – the wash of a pink sunset or pale blue of still water in a lake. The English country garden finds its way indoors, too, with brightly coloured flowers on fabrics, porcelain, carpets and stencilled motifs.

When planning a country-style interior and considering the furniture and furnishings, there is an important element of timelessness to incorporate too. In a home passed down from generation to generation this occurs perfectly naturally as each owner adds their own personal possessions and modifications, building on the existing decor. When starting from scratch, this can be easily achieved, if not by using second-hand materials and antiques, then by cleverly combining new with old or prematurely aged fabrics and furniture.

COLOUR

The colour scheme in a particular room may be dictated by one of many things: you may have a predominant item of furniture, an existing pair of curtains or a carpet which will be the starting point

Rich colours and textures that take their lead from nature will invariably look good together, yet will not appear over-co-ordinated.

for other decorative and furnishing elements. Or you may wish to use colour strategically to influence the mood and aspect of the room. Certain colours, for example, will make a room look lighter, even sunnier – which can be particularly useful in country cottages where windows may be small and rooms tend to be gloomy. The traditional plain white walls are a great lightener and a good background for richer, more detailed features; but if you find this a little too harsh, then opt instead for one of the new colour-tinted whites or a cream or yellow to brighten up a dark room. The right shade is vital and it may take some experimenting to find it. A pale lemon yellow, for example, can seem almost cool; whereas a deeper buttercup shade creates a warm, sunny feel. For cosy warmth, combine reds and oranges with a deep or navy blue, forest green, or nut brown. These darker colours will bring a room in and make it seem smaller, which can be especially useful in larger country homes where big rooms can be difficult to furnish comfortably.

If you do not relish the rich treasure-chest colours of Persian rugs, polished wood and patchwork quilts, you might prefer to go

14 *Traditional crafts and old-fashioned implements are an important element of the English country home.*

for a more low-key country style: relaxing neutrals such as cream and stone blended with several of the many shades of brown available, from palest beige to rich nutty brown. In such a scheme as this, a variety of textures will be essential to maintain interest and important contrasts. Alternatively, go for a combination of soft pastels: they are perfect for coastal country homes and offer baby blues, sugar pinks, pearl greys, palest lime greens and delicate yellows to be blended in the subtlest of contrasts. Again, remember that these shades will make a room appear larger and lighter.

PATTERN

Country rooms need traditional patterns and designs, usually featuring a lot of detail and sophisticated colour combinations: old-fashioned florals, paisleys, quirky Toile de Jouy with its rustic figures, smart stripes, or oriental themes. If you cannot buy sufficient fabric second-hand – old curtains and spare lengths of fabric at house-effects sales are an excellent way to create an instantly stylish yet lived-in look – then go to one of the old-established fabric houses which have a whole range of designs based on papers and fabrics from their archives, often drafted by famous designers from the past and which are perfect for both grand and humble country homes. However, traditional detail and good colour printing does not come cheap; if you feel such fabrics are beyond your means, then choose inexpensive sheeting, muslin or other budget fabrics for large areas and save the more expensive prints for making up tie-backs, cushions or over-cloths. Similarly, a good-quality wallpaper can work out expensive over large areas in grander rooms; consider using it on plain walls in decorative panels or choose a border print instead to add detail at dado or picture rail level. Whatever option you can afford, make sure your choice of design suits the size and scale of the room. Small prints will be lost in larger rooms that require something bold, but they do an excellent job disguising imperfect walls or oddly-shaped dimensions in a smaller one. Another important consideration when choosing patterns is not to go for too co-ordinated a look in this context: a striped design and a floral in the same colours is preferable to matching patterns of different sizes.

TEXTURE

A good variety of textures is important within a scheme, especially if your palette of colours is limited. In a country interior, the rough textures of stone, brick, wool and basketry contrast pleasantly with those of sheeny chintzes, silk-based fabrics or smooth cottons. You should look out for country-themed items and accessories that can offer interesting textures: woven rush or willow baskets for filling with logs, fir cones, magazines, or dried flowers; woollen rugs and throws for floor, wall, sofa or table; knobbly pottery on shelves and tables; and even sticks, stones, fossils, feathers and other treasures brought back from long country walks.

WALLS AND CEILINGS

Walls and ceilings can present problems in country-style dwellings; large rooms with high ceilings can be daunting and the rooms may seem impersonal and even chilly if given the wrong treatment such as an ill-advised colour or a wallpaper design that is too small. Smaller cottages can be cosier, but their walls are generally uneven and the ceilings will often be criss-crossed with heavy beams. A lumpy, bumpy wall with a discrepancy of 15cm (6in) from one side of the room to the other can be a nightmare to paper successfully and paint is usually the better option. However, if you really do prefer wallpaper, choose one with a small all-over design which makes it difficult to detect flaws – and avoid stripes at all costs. When decorating grander rooms, you should adopt the opposite attitude and think big by choosing one of the traditional bold designs printed in strong colours to prevent the paper fading into insignificance. Using matching paper borders at dado or picture rail level is another useful way of adding interest to a large or awkwardly shaped room.

If plain-painted walls seem a little dull, there are plenty of ways you can experiment with traditional ideas and finishes – and have a lot of fun into the bargain. If you have the nerve, adding a touch of colour can be remarkably effective, giving walls (and ceilings) a warm pink or honey yellow glow for example. You might even take the bold step of using a deeper shade such as russet, ochre, or tomato red – perhaps in a study or dining room, where a snug, intimate atmosphere is desirable. For a really authentic effect, you might like to try your hand at one or more traditional painting effects: they look perfect on old, uneven walls and between the beams on cottage ceilings. With the technique of wall washing, paint is applied thinly with a large brush to create an uneven blush effect. A similar effect can be achieved by mixing your own paints using pigments. Or, for a more decorative finish and perfect for disguising any imperfections, why not apply a broken paint effect? Ragging and sponging are surprisingly simple skills; you can improvise, or buy what you need in kit form from major paint companies. The beauty of these techniques is that they use two or more colours so they can be expertly tied in with other decorative or furnishing features in the room. Tone down a too-deep colour by sponging over in a paler shade; or rag-rolling in a deeper colour to add texture and design to dull walls. If you feel the walls need further decoration, there are always stencils; these can be used to

create remarkably effective borders and patterns. Another creative idea using stencils is to outline faux borders or frames for prints and pictures; or even apply them around door frames or along the line of a sloping ceiling to make a feature of an awkward room.

CURTAINS AND UPHOLSTERY

While the fireplace undoubtedly commands attention as the focal point of most rooms in country-style homes both large and small, the windows are invariably of equal importance and need to be designed and dressed carefully if the overall look is to be successful. Again, the size and style of room will dictate the kind of treatment you choose. Stately looking rooms demand something a little ostentatious: it is no good putting up a pair of unlined ready-mades and expecting them to show off a fine lead-paned window with polished oak window sills to best advantage. You need some lengths of deep coloured velvet or heavy linen/cotton mix printed with huge country-garden blooms, exotic birds or some such traditional motif, and lined – preferably interlined – to give a good hang and suggest a

Choose the right combination of furnishing features: fresh flowery fabric, dragged paint effect panelling, traditional wooden furniture and the occasional antique, and you can conjure up a country feel in any home.

sense of luxury. Grand windows need a matching pelmet sculpted into elaborate points and curves or made from stiffened fabric and draped into formal swags and tails, plus, maybe, a pair of tie-backs to keep the curtains elegantly swept back. The decorative possibilities are endless.

The more modest cottage-style window or those in attic bedrooms will often present the problem not of how to create a magnificent focal point, but what will look good yet still be practical when faced with an awkward shape or location. Often you find yourself faced with insufficient room for a rail between window and ceiling; or you may discover there is no space at the sides for bulky curtains to be pulled back. In this case, you may have to consider a special ceiling-hung track or pole, or settle for a blind and static dress curtains which have a purely decorative function at the sides of the window. Sloping dormer windows can be particularly tricky: blinds or curtains either have to be fitted within the recess, or curtains hung on a rail completely free of the window area.

Fabric also features strongly elsewhere in the room, not necessarily in a design to match that of the curtains at the window, but in similar or complementary colours and traditionally displaying intricate floral designs, smart stripes or rich paisley patterns on silk, cotton, linen or glazed chintz. There may be floor-length cloths for occasional tables, covers on sofas and chairs, pillows, cushions and lampshades, even shirred fabric along shelves and around cupboards in these materials or made from soft woollen tweeds and tartans, freshly checked cotton gingham, richly worked tapestry or cheap breezy muslin. Cloths and cushions, extra rugs, shawls and throws all help to avoid any kind of tailored look and create a seemingly unplanned and effortless impression of comfort and elegance.

FLOORING

You will not often see fitted carpets in the country-style home unless it is a tough, speckled, wool-mix berber or wall-to-wall grass or coir matting – now available in a wide range of designs and colours. More often, a hard practical flooring with rugs or carpets that can easily be pulled back for cleaning is far more the style. Cottage floors are most likely to feature stone flags, bricks, polished slate, quarry tiles or even ceramic tiles, in living rooms as well as hallways and kitchens. It is surprising the variety of patterns and designs that can be found among such basic materials. Flags will be made of local stone and can be laid in a choice of regular or random patterns; bricks and quarry tiles may be russet, ochre or even black, the bricks possibly arranged in elaborate herringbone or basketweave designs; quarry tiles and ceramics perhaps feature the traditional black and white tesselated pattern so often seen in old hallways. Sometimes the corners of the tiles have been clipped and replaced with black inserts for decorative effect.

Elsewhere elm, pine or oak floorboards may have been restored and polished. For colour and comfort there will be rugs: rich oriental carpets in the grander homes, and humble hand-made rag rugs for the simple cottage.

FURNITURE

Country-style furniture is simple and sturdy, most often left plain and polished, but sometimes painted white, cream or pastel shades of blue or yellow. New furniture, or even a matching range of faithful reproductions of traditional pieces would not look right at all. You need at least a few original items, preferably many, however aged and well-worn they might look. Junk-shop finds are ideal and they do not have to match: look out for old country chairs or the cane-seated type which are easily restored if the seats are damaged or missing.

There are, of course, classic pieces of country furniture which immediately suggest cottage style, even if they were to be arranged in a smart town flat. Firstly, there is the ubiquitous dresser in every size, shape and finish, offering valuable storage for anything from plate racks to table linen. The true antiques are expensive but reproduction versions using old pine are good value; alternatively, cheat by fitting wall shelves above a suitable cupboard. Painting the dresser in distressed pastels or traditional dark browns or greens is preferable to having glossy modern pine. Second, no country kitchen is complete without a large scrubbed pine table. For the dining room, a long narrow refectory table with carver chairs at either end is traditional. Look out for wooden settles – old church pews are frequently found in the antique shops. Also search out brass or cast iron beds, a squashy sofa and maybe a comfy chair or two. Again, it does not matter if these do not match, although you can cover them in matching fabric if you prefer. There are other traditional elements to country living that you may like to budget for if not lucky enough to own them already: a Rayburn or similar country-style stove; maybe a white roll-top bath for the bathroom; and a woodburning stove for the living room, which is a lot more economical than an open fire yet still attractive and capable of heating the whole house if linked to radiators.

COUNTRY-STYLE ACCESSORIES

A lot of glossy, expensive ornaments and accessories look out of place, even in the grander country interiors. Instead, make up collections of more personal effects, rustic antiques, or items you have found locally: plates and teapots, trinket boxes, walking sticks and umbrellas, local pottery, pictures, prints, maps and mirrors – they can all be arranged to great effect on walls, windowsills, shelves and tables. Pictures and pottery depicting farm animals or country themes seem particularly appropriate. Or make artistic arrangements of real dried herbs and flowers, of branches and cones in winter and fresh flowers in summer. There should be a few scented geraniums and herbs or similar cottage plants on the windowsill – and do not forget those country home essentials: a basket of logs for the fire, a big bowl of pot pourri and a slow ticking clock.

LIGHTING

Lighting is often forgotten when planning or designing a traditional or country-style interior, but ideally it should be one of your first considerations so that all the wiring and technical side of it can be hidden away before decorating and furnishing. Something soft and

Every shelf and free surface tends to be crammed with favourite objects, junk-shop finds and interesting collections of oddments.

relatively unobtrusive to enhance that relaxed atmosphere is preferable. That does not mean to say you cannot take advantage of the latest lighting effects; concealed spotlights, uplighters, wallwashers and recessed downlights can all work extremely well and are discreet enough not to intrude on the general atmosphere. It is a good idea to have a range of effects which can be operated individually to give full flexibility according to your mood. Certain locations demand specific treatments: good lighting in the kitchen and over the bathroom mirror, for example; over the dining table – maybe a rise-and-fall pendant light; and in the living room, strategically placed table lamps for reading or highlighting a certain corner. For more romantic evenings you cannot beat the soft flicker of old-fashioned candlelight. As well as a collection of candlesticks in wood, brass, pewter or pottery, you might like to install wall sconces in the living or dining room for intimate evenings.

CHAPTER TWO

HALLS AND STAIRWAYS

THE HALLWAY OR ENTRANCE HALL SETS the scene for your home. It makes that important first impression so, ideally, it should look good all the time and be furnished in the right kind of style. In the country-style home it must be practical and hardwearing too, a place to throw down muddy wellingtons, wet coats, walking sticks and gardening gloves. But, although durability tends to take priority over the decorative, that does not mean that the hallway should be totally lacking in charm. Even the humblest country cottage entrance is attractive in its simplicity and the combination of good honest natural materials: stone flags or well-worn quarry tiles; rough plaster walls; maybe an old wooden chair or seat for sitting on while you pull off your boots; and a row of wooden pegs for country coats.

TRADITIONAL MATERIALS

In a large hallway, there should still be an element of needing to be practical and a predominance of natural materials such as stone and timber. A harmonious blend of tough surfaces and more comfortable

1 *Sturdy wooden door*
2 *Hard surface flooring*
3 *Richly patterned rug*
4 *Wooden settle*
5 *Plain painted walls*
6 *Matching prints*
7 *Antique side table*

This splendid stencilled cabinet provides both a decorative feature and practical storage in the hallway, yet takes up relatively little space.

traditional elements works best. If there is a fireplace and it is not practical to have the fire lit, then make the most of it as a feature by placing a large arrangement of fresh or dried flowers in the grate, a basket of fir cones collected on country walks, or a stitched or painted fire screen.

WALLS AND FLOORS

You could half-panel hall walls in timber to add warmth and interest, or imitate this effect with paint or a special three-dimensional textured wallpaper. Alternatively, paint or colourwash the walls for added interest and welcome, perhaps incorporating a stencilled border or motif at picture rail or dado hieght.

For the floor you can choose from stone flags, slates, quarry tiles or ceramic floor tiles. Either leave them plain, or arrange them in a design. The most common design seen in country hallways is that of an alternate tessellated pattern: black and white if the tiles are ceramic; russet and black for quarries. Both types of tile are also available with clipped corners and coloured inserts (usually black) for a traditional effect.

FURNITURE

There may be room for a few pieces of furniture in larger halls, such as a hallstand for coats, and perhaps a wooden settle with lift-up seat for storing gloves and overshoes. An old table, with or without some kind of cloth – not a fine cotton print but a piece of tapestry or woollen cloth – is useful for letters or displaying a few items such as a pot plant, an arrangement of flowers or a bowl of pot pourri. A stand for keeping umbrellas, walking sticks and fishing rods in order

is always useful, as is a rack for storing boots tidily. Incorporating some kind of mirror in a hallway is important; it should be as large as possible and in a heavy frame. An antique mirror may be expensive to buy but ornate picture frames can be bought quite cheaply at auction sales and junk shops, then the picture removed and a piece of mirror glass inserted in its place.

These elements can be adapted for smaller hallways, too, depending on what you have have room for. They are typical of country homes where a relaxed and comfortable atmosphere belies an essentially well organized and practical style for living.

The uneven effect of colour washing is perfect for adding warmth and interest to plain walls.

PROJECTS

You will need

*

- Sealant (optional)
- Emulsion paint
- Paint roller
- Water
- Paint tray or kettle
- Wide wall paintbrush

1 *First prepare the wall. If it has been distempered in the past, you must scrub off all trace of any loose, chalky finish and seal the surface with a proprietary sealant. Now, using a paint roller, apply an undiluted base coat of emulsion paint in the colour of your choice. If the base coat is white, washing a pastel shade over it will have an excellent lightening effect;*

COLOURWASHED WALLS

Wall washing with diluted paint produces an uneven faded effect with a translucent finish which is perfect for country-style interiors, producing an instantly aged and mellow appearance reminiscent of the old-fashioned distemper. You can use ordinary household emulsion paint which offers an excellent, wide range of colours. It is also easy to apply and dries quickly. Use a silk finish for a lovely translucent effect, or matt vinyl paint to create a soft appearance.

alternatively, using a deeper colour for the basecoat and a lighter shade for the wash will create a subtle but rich three-dimensional finish.

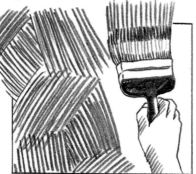

2 *When the base coat has completely dried, mix up your chosen wash colour by diluting paint with water in a paint tray or kettle wide enough to accommodate a wide wall brush. You will find instructions on the tin advising the best proportion of paint to water — it is vital to get this right if you want to achieve an attractive finish and avoid ugly runs and drips. Apply the colourwash and allow the paint to dry completely. It is important that you do not try to brush out the paint evenly, rather use the brush in random directions with a cross-hatching technique to*

produce a distressed effect of uneven colour depth. With this first coat it is not necessary to cover the background completely and some areas should be left exposed. When the first wash coat is dry, mix more paint, diluting to the same proportions and apply a second coat using the same technique and a wide wall brush, this time covering the entire wall.

STRIPPED AND VARNISHED FURNITURE

Stripping, restaining and then varnishing an old item of furniture can transform a junk-shop bargain into a fine-looking piece, perfect for an English country interior. Always check that your piece is free from active woodworm. Clear varnish is available in a choice of a gloss, satin or matt finish and produces protection without spoiling the natural finish of the wood. Alternatively, if you wish to add a touch of colour, such as red, blue, green or grey, use a ready colour-tinted woodstain or varnish. Remember that the more coats you apply, the deeper will be the colour.

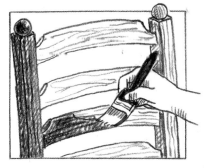

You will need

- Protective gloves
- Newspaper
- Paint stripping gel, solution or paste, or hot-air gun
- Paint scraper
- Shavehook
- Soft cloth
- Sandpaper
- Varnish
- Varnish brush
- White spirit

and left, according to the manufacturer's instructions. When the paint begins to bubble, scrape it off with a scraper or a shavehook. Alternatively, you could use a hot-air gun. The gun operates rather like a hair dryer to soften and bubble the old paint. Work from the bottom to the top so that the rising heat heats the paint above.

3 When dry, varnish the piece. Apply the varnish thinly: several thin coats are always preferable to one thick one. Work only along the grain of the wood, brushing the varnish out evenly to the edges and finishing off with a single upward stroke to avoid any runs. When dry, rub the wood down gently with sandpaper and clean with white spirit before applying a second coat in the same way. Two coats are usually enough for furniture.

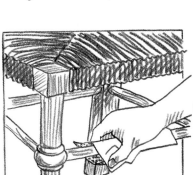

2 When the piece of furniture is strippped, wash it down with white spirit to remove any loose paint or chemical residue. Then sand it thoroughly to lift any last scraps of paint and to produce a fine finish. Always rub in the direction of the grain to prevent ugly scrapes and scratches. Wipe down again and allow to dry.

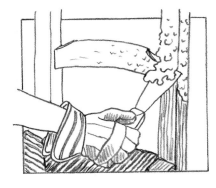

1 When stripping furniture, always wear protective gloves and work in a well-ventilated room. Stand the piece of furniture on plenty of layers of newspaper to protect your floor. Then strip off any old paint or finish with a chemical stripper applied in layers

CHAPTER THREE

DINING ROOMS

ONLY LARGER ENGLISH COUNTRY HOMES and farmhouses are usually lucky enough to enjoy the luxury of a separate dining room. In more modest houses and most cottages, a scrubbed pine table in the kitchen or a polished gateleg table in a corner of the living room must suffice.

The right kind of wood or a pretty cloth can help incorporate an eating area into other rooms quite comfortably, if you take care to match the area to its surrounding furnishing scheme. To give the table more prominence and highlight the area during special meals, you can always use moveable folding screens – decorated in fabric, wallpaper or old-fashioned collage scraps – or devise a lighting system that offers a variety of individually operated effects around the room. You should be able to soften a bright all-round light by dimming the general lights and keeping the table spotlit. This can be achieved through a combination of wall lights, uplighters and downlights strategically positioned so that you can have light

1 Corner cupboard
2 Wooden dresser
3 Best china on display
4 Solid wooden refectory table
5 Carver chairs

6 Polished country chairs
7 Candles provide soft lighting
8 Turkey rug
9 Polished floorboards

exactly when and where you want it at the flick of a switch or turn of a dimmer control. A rise-and-fall lamp positioned directly over the table is an excellent device for combination dining rooms; it gives the diners good light and can be raised or lowered according to your mood. Nor should you forget the effect of humble candles: their soft flickering light is flattering both to you and the room, and they can be placed exactly where you need them. In any case, an interesting selection of candlesticks are essential country-style accessories, combining as they do the practical with the ornamental. Start a collection in wood, pewter, brass, silver or ceramic, to be displayed on your dresser, mantelpiece or table.

FURNITURE

The separate dining room can afford to be more indulgent: again, a flexible lighting system is important to match the mood of the meal – and candlelight can be extended to permanent wall-mounted sconces as well as candlesticks. The classic formal country dining room has a long, narrow refectory table, the top traditionally made from a single piece of wood, with comfortable carvers at either end and high-backed chairs or bench seating along the sides to seat plenty of friends and family. There may be room for a few additional pieces of country furniture: the dresser is another classic and an excellent way to display your china, brass, pewter or silver attractively. The buffet table or sideboard can also be used to display items or it can be equally useful for holding dishes during the meal. If you do a lot of entertaining, it is worth converting a sideboard or cupboard into a warming cupboard for plates and dishes.

WALLS

This is one room in the country home where a painted finish or papered elegance such as stripes is generally preferable to fussy florals. A colourwash or broken paint effect such as rag-rolling can look particularly effective by candlelight. A very formal effect can be achieved by panelling – or more often half panelling – the room. There are companies who are able to do this, or you can buy whole

rooms of antique panelling, carefully removed from old properties and stored at architectural salvage yards.

WINDOWS

If the dining room is mainly for evening use, the window has less prominence too, leaving the table as focal point. Choosing curtain fabric to match the wallpaper or selecting plain velvet or linen will help play it down. However, where wall space on either side is limited, a curtain blind, whether a pleated Roman type or the fussier Austrian blind, might be the best option. Alternatively, you could dispense with any kind of window treatment altogether in the dining room and simply use old-fashioned wooden shutters to shut out the night.

A country-style dining room that is used daily rather than

In larger rooms a rise-and-fall lamp helps to focus attention on the table and provides good light for diners.

This is young country style: fabric and paint have been combined to make this sunny breakfast room both pretty and practical.

mainly for entertaining or for special meals can be given more of a family feel with a generously sized pine table and fresh flowery curtains at the window – a style reminiscent of the old breakfast room, especially if the room catches the early morning sun.

Whatever style you choose, the room needs a practical yet attractive flooring: stripped boards look good but can be a little noisy. Wall-to-wall sisal or tiles – a tesselated black and white design is traditional – are equally suitable.

$\mathcal{P}$ROJECTS

You will need
❊

- Paper
- Pencil
- Scissors
- Felt pen
- Foam (about 2.5cm, 1in thick)
- Calico or strong cotton
- Needle and thread
- Fabric
- Tape measure
- Tailor's chalk
- Ruler
- Pins
- Sewing machine
- Iron
- Piping cord

TIE-ON CUSHION PAD

Tie-on cushion pads add a touch of comfort to simple wooden chairs intended for the dining room or kitchen and, if you use fabric left over from making your blinds or curtains, they are economical to make and will fit the overall scheme of the room beautifully. Using cushions is also a clever way of making an odd assortment of similar-sized chairs look like a set. You could paint or stain the chairs the same colour to reinforce the effect.

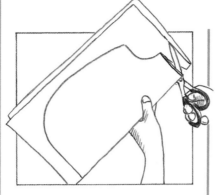

1 *You can buy ready-cut foam pads but, for a good fit, make a pattern of the chair seat by placing a sheet of paper on the seat and drawing around it. Cut out the paper and fold it in half lengthwise to make sure both sides are equal. Mark where the ties should come.*

2 *Use the paper pattern and a felt pen to mark the shape onto a piece of foam. Cut out the shape and wrap it with a piece of calico or*

strong cotton fabric to protect it from wear, sewing to secure it. Cut out two pieces of fabric using the same paper pattern but this time allowing 12mm (½in) all around for seams. Using tailor's chalk, mark the position for the ties on the reverse of what will be the top piece.

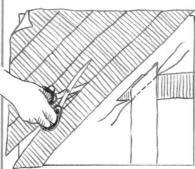

3 *Prepare a length of bias binding for covering the piping cord. Take a square or near-square piece of matching or contrasting fabric. Using a ruler, mark parallel lines diagonally across the fabric, 38mm (1½in) apart. Cut the strips. Join by laying two strips, right sides together, at right angles. Stitch across the diagonal lines as shown, press open the seams and trim.*

continued over ➤

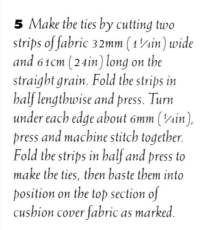

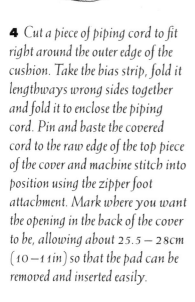

4 Cut a piece of piping cord to fit right around the outer edge of the cushion. Take the bias strip, fold it lengthways wrong sides together and fold it to enclose the piping cord. Pin and baste the covered cord to the raw edge of the top piece of the cover and machine stitch into position using the zipper foot attachment. Mark where you want the opening in the back of the cover to be, allowing about 25.5 – 28cm (10 – 11in) so that the pad can be removed and inserted easily.

5 Make the ties by cutting two strips of fabric 32mm (1¼in) wide and 61cm (24in) long on the straight grain. Fold the strips in half lengthwise and press. Turn under each edge about 6mm (¼in), press and machine stitch together. Fold the strips in half and press to make the ties, then baste them into position on the top section of cushion cover fabric as marked.

6 Pin and baste the front section of the cover to the back with right sides together. Machine stitch all around, leaving the opening unstitched. Trim the seams and clip any curves to ensure they lie flat. Turn the cover right side out and insert the foam. Slip-stitch the opening closed to finish.

DRIED FLOWER WREATH

Dried flower arrangements in pots and boxes, buckets, baskets or vases are used extensively for decoration around the English country-style home, and they can be used as a delightful furnishing accessory for walls and ceilings too. Circular wreaths can be permanently fixed to walls and doors, while flowery swags and garlands are the perfect decoration along mantelpieces, dresser shelves, beams and the tops of wardrobes. It is more fun if you can dry your own plants and flowers, gleaned from garden and hedgerow. This not only produces a more interesting variety of flowers and herbs than the ones you can buy, but also provides a further decorative possibility if hung from racks and hooks above windows or below beams. Construction materials are easily purchased from florist's shops.

to organize a symmetrical design. Using florist's wire, wire the stems of the dried material so that it can be fastened onto the ring. Flowers may be wired individually; herbs, foliage, small flowers, buds and other plants can be fastened together and wired as sprigs or bunches. Place a medium wire alongside the stems and bend it over about halfway up. Twist it around the stems to secure them, leaving enough to wire the arrangement into the wreath.

You will need

- Wire ring base
- Sphagnum moss
- Florist's wire
- Selection of dried flowers and herbs
- Ribbons (optional)

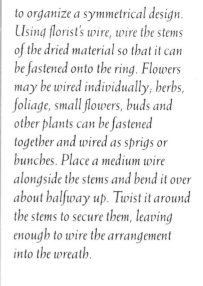

2 An attractively balanced wreath is best planned in advance. Lay the dried flowers out on a flat surface so that you get some idea of how they look together and

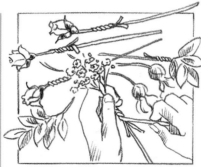

3 Insert the wired ends of the flowers and sprigs into the mossy ring to cover the ring completely. If desired, finish the wreath with ribbons and bows.

1 To make a circular wreath, neatly cover a wire ring base with tightly packed sphagnum moss. Hold this in place by winding a length of florist's wire over the ring and tucking the loose end under the moss.

$\mathcal{L}$IVING ROOMS

THE ENGLISH COUNTRY-STYLE LIVING ROOM is cosy and warm in winter, yet cool and inviting in summer; in our imagination it remains the perfect place to 'take tea' or enjoy a post-Sunday lunch snooze. Nor does the reality often disappoint. Much of this room's charm lies in that wonderfully relaxed atmosphere which seduces us into the armchair or onto the windowseat to idle away a few hours. Yet that all-important anti-stress factor is actually quite easy to achieve. Your decorative scheme should have a timeless quality composed of a few (genuine or mocked-up) antiques, the slightly lived-in look of faded or scuffed furnishings, and, above all, comfortable furniture, pleasing shapes and colours incorporating country themes and textures, and lots of rugs, covers, cushions, cloths and drapes to create an easy-on-the-eye, even crumpled, appearance. What you want to avoid is any impression of over-co-ordination and hard-edged chic – it may be smart but it is never relaxing.

1 *Heavily beamed ceiling*
2 *Open fireplace*
3 *Comfortable seating*
4 *Oriental carpet*

5 *Pretty floral fabric*
6 *Antique furniture*
7 *Subtle lighting effects*
8 *Exposed brickwork*

In both summer and winter, the fireplace creates the perfect focal point in the living room.

FIREPLACES

The focal point of many cottage living rooms is the fireplace. It may be little more than a space in the wall containing an open grate but the flicker of a live flame, the 'hands-on' experience of putting on rough-hewn logs and the lingering scent of woodsmoke are essential elements of the rural idyll. Often a fine old fireplace will be hidden behind a newer, fancier feature and opening it up will not only give your room more country credibility but will make it larger too. This is particularly true where the fireplace turns out to be an inglenook which can be large enough to stand in, and possibly incorporates seats, shelves or a bread oven in the sides. If you are opening up a new fireplace it is important that you have the chimney checked and, if necessary, swept and repaired before you light a fire. Excess smoke in the room is irritating, but, worse, a leaking chimney can release toxic fumes into the house.

For a grander English country-style look, you can choose

ornamental fireplace surrounds featuring fluted columns or detailed carvings in wood, metal, plaster, stone or marble. Fireplaces can be restored to their former glory by purchasing a good reproduction version or a rescued original from a salvage yard. For any kind of replacement to look right, it is important that you take the time to research the correct period and choose the right size and height in proportion to the room.

An alternative that is better than an open fire in many ways yet offering virtually all the same aesthetic advantages as a grate is a woodburning stove. There are very many sizes and styles to choose from that will suit a country-style setting and they can be fitted into an existing fireplace or sited anywhere in the room providing you can supply a suitable flue. A stove is far more heat-efficient than an open fire. Many are extremely attractive and some have large doors which can be opened up giving you a view of the live flame. If you want the look but not the hassle of handling solid fuel, you can even buy gas-fired flame-effect models which operate at the flick of a switch.

Softer blues can have a warming effect. This comfortable chair and writing table have created a charming corner by a sunny window.

WINDOWS

English cottage windows tend to be small, often deep-set on account of thick walls, and maybe lead-paned. To reproduce the look of these quaint cottage windows, the curtains should be simple in style, with a narrow fabric pelmet, plain ribbon or cord tie-backs and rustic wooden or metal curtain poles. For a living room which has large windows, choose generous and ornately styled pelmets,

tie-backs, tassels and other trims to maximize its impact. A large window will also demand bolder treatment with large, bright print curtains.

One of the nicest features of English country cottages is the windowseat, with plenty of cushions and a good view of the countryside; if you are not lucky enough to have an original windowseat, you could always create one and incorporate storage such as bookshelves or cupboards or even a radiator (with ornamental grille) beneath.

WALLS AND FLOORS

A fitted carpet on the floor can appear out of keeping with an English country-style look. But, if you feel a hard surface such as stone flags or quarry tiles is a bit spartan in the living room, then there are plenty of more comfortable country-style options. Coir or sisal matting can be fitted wall to wall or left as mats and it has a wonderfully natural appearance. You can buy it in a variety of patterns and even different colours. Add warmth, colour and comfort with rugs: jewel-like Persian rugs (they need not be new and are easily found at auction sales); the paler pastels of soft dhurries (hand-made Indian cotton rugs); or knobbly rag rugs – the traditional cottager's comfort for the floor. Alternatively, you might prefer thick Chinese or Indian carpets offering deeply sculpted pastels or an intricately woven combination of rich shades, chosen according to the room's general colour scheme. Of course, these rugs look as good on the walls as they do on the floor. Like tapestry, they offer depth of colour and interesting textures and, incidentally, they are an excellent way to cover up a poor wall surface.

The walls in a living room can be plain, especially where you have lots of pattern and texture in the surrounding fabrics and other

Above: Cool cream walls are the neutral background for rich russets, browns and old golds, which respond well to flickering firelight.
Opposite: An old ethnic rug like this glowing example could easily be copied onto canvas.

The simplest object might be the inspiration for a complete country scheme. Here the dark blue decoration on a rustic jug has been picked up in a wall stencil and glass painting.

features, or where you want a plain background to set off a collection of pictures, plates, or wall-hung artefacts. You can get away with quite deep shades for cosy rooms but if you would rather create more of a light and airy look, a paler colour or even white would be better. The type of paint is important too: a hand-mixed pigment-based colour such as milk paint gives an uneven yet authentic finish. Alternatively, you might prefer to choose something a little more decorative in the living room, in which case you could choose a broken paint effect such as sponging or wall washing, or a traditional decorative technique like stencilling.

High-ceilinged living rooms might need a different treatment. You could use a wide paper border or half panelling to break up the area and visually reduce a high ceiling. Painting the ceiling a dark colour will also effectively lower it; if you prefer a lofty effect, use paler pastels and vertical stripes on the walls. If blazer stripes look too formal, there are many floral designs incorporating a stripe or ribbon which will create the same lengthening effect. Pick out elaborate features, such as plaster mouldings or an Adam-style ceiling, in Wedgwood colours to emphasize their fine detail.

FURNITURE

Furniture should be chosen with comfort in mind: squashy sofas in floral cotton, tweed, tartan or paisley; footstools, high-backed chairs to keep draughts off your neck; occasional tables loaded with books, treasures and table lamps. All can be purchased second-hand and recovered or at least given a new lease of life with loose covers, cushions, cloths, shawls and throws. These will only enhance the country atmosphere and are also a useful way to mellow new furniture. Rustic-style furniture can be quite elegant, but it always has a sense of robustness which avoids the delicate finish and detail of salon-style antiques.

$\mathcal{P}$ROJECTS

LINED LAMPSHADE

Covering your own lampshade is quite time-consuming but easy enough to do and very rewarding. The lined shade will be far superior to one you can buy in the shops and you can have exactly the shape and finish you want, even matching other furnishings in the room if the fabric is suitable. The fabric has to be reasonably lightweight to allow the light to shine through and for the seams not to be too bulky. The lining material can be any pastel shade although white will naturally reflect maximum light. A thimble is necessary to protect fingers while hand sewing.

You will need

- Lampshade frame
- Tape measure
- 12mm (½in) cotton tape
- Fabric
- Sharp scissors
- Cotton or satin lining fabric
- Fine sharp needles and thread
- Steel pins
- Thimble
- Pencil
- Iron
- Trimming, such as braid or tassels
- Fabric adhesive

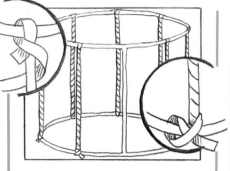

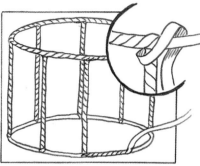

1 *Cover the frame with tape so that you have something to stitch the fabric to. To estimate how much tape you require, measure the circumference of the two rings and the length of all the struts, then double this figure. Tape each strut separately, beginning where it joins the top ring and making the first pass over the ring to secure the tape. Wrap the tape diagonally around the strut, keeping it tight and free from any rucks or wrinkles. It should overlap itself by around 3mm (⅛in) to avoid any gaps. When you get to the bottom ring, fasten the tape by winding it over the ring and back through the loop to make a half knot and pull it tight. All the struts except for one should be taped in this manner.*

2 *Starting at the untaped strut, begin taping the top ring, wrapping the tape over itself to secure it as before and making a figure-of-eight around the top of each strut as you pass it. When you have worked your way back round to the bare strut, work down it, then pass the tape around the bottom ring, making a figure-of-eight around each strut as before. When finished, the end of the tape can be folded under about 6mm (¼in) and hand-stitched to the outside of the taped ring.*

continued over ➤

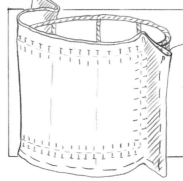

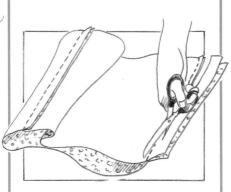

44

3 From your main fabric, cut a rectangle with a length equal to the circumference of the frame, plus 15cm (6in); its width must equal the hieght of the frame plus 7.5cm (3in). Use the same dimensions to cut the lining material. With right sides facing, fold the main fabric in half and baste the cut edges together to prevent it slipping. Wearing a thimble, lay the doubled fabric against half the frame and pin it into place against two facing struts to achieve exactly the right shape. The straight grain of the fabric must run vertically up the shade. Insert the pins inwards along each strut, gently easing out any fullness of the fabric to the sides as you go. Then pin the fabric to the top and bottom rings in the same way, smoothing out any wrinkles and pulling tight from top to bottom to get the tightest possible fit.

4 Mark the seam line down the side of each strut with a series of pencil dots between the pins. Carefully remove the fabric from the frame, baste and then stitch along the line of pencilled dots. Trim away the excess fabric at the sides to within 6mm (¼in) of the stitching line. Press the seams to one side (not open) and turn the shade the right way out. Prepare the lining material in the same way but stitching the seams to about 3mm (⅛in) inside the pencil lines.

5 Position the main fabric over the frame, making sure that the seams line up neatly with the vertical struts so that they will be less visible when the light shines behind them. Pin the top and bottom edges to the rings without allowing the side seams to slip out of place. Oversew the top and bottom edges of the cover onto the outside edges of the taped rings using doubled thread and tiny stitches. Trim away any surplus fabric as close to the line of stitching as possible.

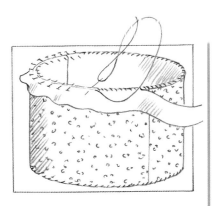

6 *Position the lining material inside the shade, matching the seams with those of the outer cover and placing lining and cover wrong sides together. Pin to the top and bottom rings and ease out any wrinkles as before. To allow it to lie flat, slit the fabric around the gimbal. Overstitch along the top and bottom edges, keeping the stitches small and positioning them as closely as possible to the outer edge so that they will be concealed behind your chosen trim. Cut away any excess fabric with sharp scissors.*

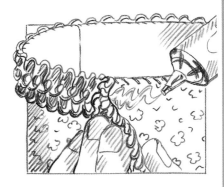

7 *Finally, glue a co-ordinated or contrasting trim around the top and bottom edges of the shade, to hide your stitching line and provide a decorative feature.*

ZIPPED CUSHION COVER

An abundance of cushions almost epitomizes the comfortable English country-style look and, although they are quite expensive to buy, new cushion covers are very easy and relatively inexpensive to make yourself, using fabric remnants or material to match other furnishings such as curtains. If you have a lot of small scraps, you could even make a patchwork cushion. For the cushions to look properly plump and inviting, the cover should be made to the same size or slightly smaller than the cushion pad.

45

You will need

- Square cushion pad
- Tape measure
- Fabric
- Piping cord (optional)
- Pins
- Needle and thread
- Sewing machine
- Iron
- Zip, 10cm (4in) shorter than the length of the cover

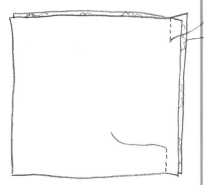

1 *Measure the cushion pad with a tape measure and to these measurements add 2.5cm (1in) to allow for seams plus sufficient extra for covering the piping. Cut out two pieces of fabric to this size. To estimate the amount of piping cord needed, measure all the way around the edge of the cushion cover and add 2.5cm (1in) for the overlap. Place the two pieces of fabric together, right sides facing and matching the raw edges. Pencil a seam line about 12mm (½in) from the edge, pin, baste and machine-stitch 5cm (2in) in from each end. Press open the two stitched sections plus the unstitched section between them. From the right side, slip-stitch the opening together roughly along the folded edges.*

2 *Centre the zip under the opening, then pin and baste in place. Using the zipper foot on your sewing machine and working from the right side of the fabric, top-stitch the zip in place, keeping your stitching line about 3mm (⅛in) from the teeth of the zip.*

continued over ➤

Stitch across the ends of the zip to join the lines of topstitching, keeping as close to the end of the teeth as possible. Press seam allowances around the zip and open the zip a little way.

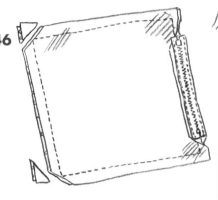

4 *Turn the cover the right side out and insert the cushion pad, making sure it reaches right into the corners of the cover. If you like, piping cord, trimming braid, fringing or tassels can be chosen in complementary colours and slip-stitched around the edge of the cover before the pad is inserted.*

3 *Turn the cover the wrong side out and pin, baste and machine-stitch around the remaining three sides, allowing 12mm (½in) for the seam. Use zigzag stitch along the raw edges to neaten and prevent fraying. On the fourth side, pin, baste and machine stitch about 5cm (2in) in from each end. Clip the corners and press the seams to prevent bunching when the cover is eventually turned the right way out.*

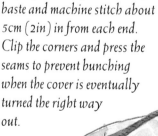

PAINTED CANVAS RUG

Cottagers have always been renowned for their ingenuity and creative penny-saving ideas and this traditional canvas or oil-cloth rug is surprisingly easy yet tremendously satisfying to make. Depending on your patience and level of skill, you can use this technique to imitate any kind of rug from simple dhurries to more complex oriental rugs and kelims. Providing you apply several coats of varnish and use padding underneath, the rug should survive considerable wear and tear without cracking or wearing. Alternatively, you could hang it on the wall!

You will need
❋

- Thick cotton canvas
- Acrylic gesso
- Housepainter's brush
- Tacks
  - Large board, craft table or frame
  - Chalk or soft pencil
- Graph paper
- Acrylic paints
- Artist's brushes
- Matt or eggshell varnish
- Varnish brush
- Venetian red oil colour (optional)
- Padded underlay
- PVA-based adhesive

onto the prepared canvas using chalk or soft pencil. A complicated geometric design may need to be drawn up on graph paper first, then transferred to the canvas using templates. Alternatively, use geometric patterns and classic rug motifs within a series of borders.

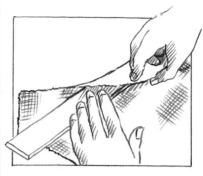

1 Buy a piece of thick cotton canvas the size you require the rug to be, remembering to allow for turning under about 5 – 7.5cm (2 – 3in) all around when it is finished. Canvas is available in a choice of widths and coarse or fine weaves. To prepare it for painting, apply three to four coats of acrylic gesso, allowing the canvas to dry thoroughly between coats. This will seal the fibres and stiffen the canvas. The raw canvas will be rather absorbent so dilute the first coat.

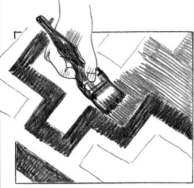

3 Apply the paint, filling in one colour at a time – this is where a plan or chart is useful – on complex patterns. Simpler rugs might employ an all-over background colour with motifs added when this is dry. To reproduce the effect of a rug's weave and texture, mix the paint to a fairly runny consistency and apply with a square-ended brush, keeping to the same direction across the grain and allowing the depth of colour to vary. Different colours should be allowed to blend slightly while still wet to avoid any hard lines. Thinning the paint will achieve an authentic worn effect here and there.

4 When the rug is complete, remove the tacks and apply four coats of varnish for protection, allowing the rug to dry completely between coats. If liked, add a little Venetian red oil paint to the varnish to produce an antiqued effect. Turn under the edges – you will have to get it right first time as the edges will crack – and glue the canvas to a padded underlay using a PVA-based adhesive.

2 The canvas needs to be stretched taut while you work on it to provide a good surface and prevent it warping out of shape. Tack it onto a large board, craft table, frame or to the floor, whichever is most practical. Mark your design

KITCHENS

THE KITCHEN REALLY IS THE HUB AND HEART of the English country home, where family and friends spend the majority of their time soaking up the warmth and comfort of that absolutely essential country accessory – the range or solid-fuel stove such as the multi-ovened Aga or Rayburn. This is not just where home cooking takes place, but also gossip, homework, play and general relaxing. The country-style kitchen often has to double as an informal dining room and, where there is space for a small settee or settle, as a secondary living room, too. While the kitchen tends to be rather small in many cottage kitchens – often little more than a ship's galley – the existence of a separate scullery to take all those bulky utility items, such as a washing machine, dryer and freezer, and a walk-in pantry or larder for storing tins, packets and jars, helps you to organize what space there is more usefully. The English country-style kitchen tends to be a scaled-down version of the classic English farmhouse kitchen: natural pine units, a big white Belfast sink, and quarry tiles on the floor is everyone's instant image, but in

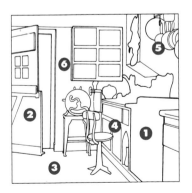

1 *Country cooker*
2 *Stable door*
3 *Polished brick floor*
4 *Stripped pine units*
5 *Wall-hung implements and utensils*
6 *Plain painted walls*

Even a generously sized country kitchen is busy with detail and buzzing with activity: here beam-hung pots and baskets, a dresser laden with crocks, and old church pews given new life as kitchen settles, are evidence of a much used and loved room.

fact there are many traditonal options and variations depending on the size and scale of the room.

APPLIANCES

The Aga/Rayburn is at the heart of the English kitchen, providing as it does a variety of cooking facilities, as well as a means of drying washing, providing hot water and possibly heating most of the radiators, too. But the mess and toil of solid fuel is no longer obligatory; these sturdy workbeasts are now available with the option of being powered by gas, oil and even electricity, and come in a range of sizes and rich enamelled colours. This will be the starting point for many kitchen schemes, although in very small rooms it is worth bearing in mind that if the stove is to be kept running all year, which many are, it will be too hot to sit in there comfortably. Other appliances such as the fridge or dishwasher do not sit as comfortably in the country scheme; if you do not have a

If you feel a predominance of varnished wood is unsuitable for smaller kitchens, cupboards and units can be painted white or a pastel shade to create a lighter yet still traditional feel reinforced by the right rustic accessories.

separate utility room for these appliances, they are best hidden away behind fake doors designed to match your cupboards or units.

FURNITURE

Country kitchen classics include the wooden dresser, which should be packed with plates, cups, pewter, brass, treen and any other treasured items you wish to keep on display. This wonderfully useful piece of furniture can be antique or reproduction, and any size from a tiny two-door unit to something that takes up a whole wall and comes complete with a full range of tiny drawers and dog kennel. The dresser might be in a finish to match that of your other cupboards, perhaps polished oak or pine. Or it might be painted an antiqued pastel or dark green or brown, maybe with additional hand-painted motifs such as fruit or flowers. You can easily fake a dresser if you cannot afford to buy one or have failed to find the right size to fit the space available (remember to allow for height as

For a softer look or where the budget will not stretch to new units, take off the cupboard doors and use shirred fabric – a cottage classic.

well as width and depth where ceilings are low). Simply fit a row of shelves to the wall above a cupboard and paint or stain them to match.

Other useful cupboards might be incorporated as fitted units and these could be in one of many timber finishes from pine, oak and chestnut to aged 'limed' finishes and painted colours. Pale blue, yellow, or cream have a lighter, less claustrophobic effect than dark wood. Hand-painted distressed finishes are also popular for achieving that old-fashioned country look and woodgraining, paint washing or stippling are easily applied. Work surfaces can be polished marble, slate, timber or tiles – or if it is the look rather than the function that is important, a man-made imitation of one of these materials. While fitted units are useful for maximizing space in smaller kitchens, a truly rustic atmosphere is better conjured up by an unfitted scheme combining a dresser and work station with a variety of shelves and cupboards for storage.

Also essential if you have the space is the scrubbed pine table, preferably some well-used antique with a selection of chairs around it. These need not be a matching set but if you prefer a co-ordinated look, then sale-room oddments can always be painted or stained in matching colours and fitted with tie-on cushions for extra comfort. Another classic is the large white-enamelled Belfast sink which is still available new if you cannot find one at the salvage yards. Generously proportioned, this looks far more authentic than any stainless steel or enamelled double-drainer unit and is deep enough to take the largest pans. With a Belfast sink it is important to fit the draining board carefully so that any excess water drains away easily; solid timber or some similar natural material always looks the most in keeping but must be efficiently sealed against moisture.

A pretty checked fabric prevents this frilled blind from looking too prissy, yet retains that essential country feel.

WINDOWS

You must think of practicality when considering the window treatment in a country-style kitchen. Fresh gingham check or pretty floral curtains may have the right feel but make sure they will not get in the way of cooking and food preparation. Choose a roller or frilly blind where space is limited or keep curtains out of the way with tie-backs. When choosing fabrics, remember that kitchen curtains will have to be washed frequently. Since net curtains are not really practical and they do not create the right effect, an attractive and traditional alter-native for kitchen (and dining

Simple animal shapes and figures can be taken from other features and applied to your painted plate to great effect.

room) windows and which offer an element of privacy are café curtains. These are made to cover the lower half of the window and hang from a decorative rod or pole.

ACCESSORIES

Pots, pans and smaller handy utensils need not be hidden away in the country kitchen. They can be displayed on open shelving or hung from wall racks, especially if you have a fine collection of handsome enamelled or cast iron pans or matching stainless steel whisks, sieves, spoons and servers. There are even special ceiling-mounted racks in timber or metal particularly designed for holding pans or drying laundry. Look out for wooden boxes, racks and rails for storing other kitchen essentials such as wooden spoons, kitchen paper, sharp knives or eggs, then fill up any spare space with wall-hung plates, salt-dough figures, old prints of country scenes or farmyard animals. Finally, you can hang dried herbs, flowers or strings of hops from the ceiling.

$\mathcal{P}$ROJECTS

WOODGRAIN FINISH

If you cannot afford to replace all your kitchen units with solid wood country-style cupboards, or you have an old dresser or cupboard that is not worth stripping, you could always try your hand at transforming them with woodgraining. All it costs is a little paint and a lot of patience. The technique may take a little practice to get right, but the final effect can be a remarkable *trompe-l'oeil*. Alternatively, if you would prefer a more colourful traditional finish, the units could be dragged (a tinted glaze is applied over an eggshell basecoat using a rag or special brush called a flogger); or combed (a tinted glaze applied over an eggshell basecoat is then scraped with special decorator's combs to make different patterns).

You will need
❈

- Duster
- Cloth
- Primer
- Housepainter's brushes
- Tinted eggshell-finish basecoat
- Tinted oil glaze
- Sponge
- Softening brush
- Artist's oil colour
- Artist's brush

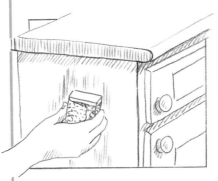

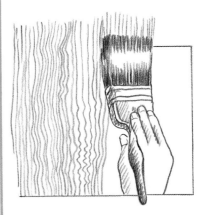

1 *Before you start, it is a good idea to familiarize yourself with the particular wood you are intending to imitate. Find a piece of pine, oak or mahogany and study the graduations of colour, the way the grain is marked and any special distinctions such as the knotty effect of pine. Prepare the surface to be painted by dusting, cleaning and priming it. Then apply an eggshell-finish basecoat in the lightest colour found in your chosen timber. Allow to dry thoroughly.*

2 *Apply a transparent oil glaze, which should be chosen in a darker shade of the basecoat colour — study your real-life sample to check what colour range you should be considering. Apply it with a housepainter's brush, stroking and wriggling the brush as you go until you develop a technique that effectively reproduces the grain of the timber you have in mind.*

continued over ➤

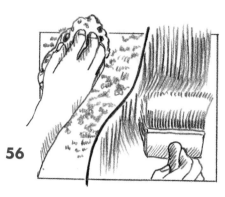

3 *There are various extra 'tools' you can use to imitate the grain. Try dabbing with a natural sponge to produce a speckled effect; a wide brush with thick, soft bristles can be used to pull the glaze in a variety of directions; even*

knuckles and fingers may come in useful for producing 'fingerprint' markings like the fingermark knots to be found in pine.

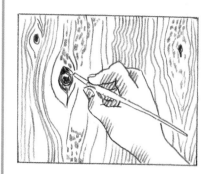

4 *Other typical markings can be reproduced more finely using artist's oil colour and a fine artist's brush. Or use a crayon to draw knot holes in the woodgrain.*

PAINTED PLATE

Plates are not just a practical element of the country home: they are an essential decorative feature, whether on the wall, dresser or shelf. While old plates are quite easy to come by in junk shops and antique centres, the prettiest may be quite costly, and it can be expensive to build up a collection for a decorative display. Painting your own plates can be great fun and much cheaper. You can buy special ceramic paints which are 'proved' in the oven to prevent them chipping off and these allow you free rein to decorate plain white plates with flowers, fruit, animals – and even country scenes – depending on your artistic prowess. However, if you find these paints difficult to find locally, you could always imitate the colourful bargeware of the last century by painting enamelled metal plates with modeller's enamels. Both plates and paints can be purchased for very litle outlay at hardware stores.

You will need
❋

- Enamelled plate
- Spray paint (optional)
- Enamel paints
- Newspaper or card
- Artist's brushes

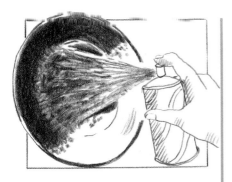

1 Enamelled plates are traditionally sold as white with a navy rim, but if you prefer to give your plate more depth of colour and a deeper background for painted patterns, spray it with special enamel paint: deep blue or dark green are the most effective background shades. Spray evenly in a well-ventilated room and leave to dry.

3 To create quick roses, sketch a ball shape by using your brush in a circular motion. Paint a series of smaller circles around the outside to make the petals. Add a darker shade to give the impression of light and shade.

4 When the flowers are dry, add the leaves and stalks using flat brushstrokes and green paint. To create a three-dimensional effect, paint half of each leaf in a darker shade. Wait for the paint to dry, then mix blue with the green and use a fine-pointed brush to apply the veins; the secret is not to take them right to the edge of the leaves.

2 Practise painting floral motifs on a piece of newspaper or card. Individual petals and leaves are applied with a single flick of the brush. Loading the brush with two or three colours produces a shaded, three-dimensional effect. Daisies are easily created using simple tear-shaped strokes to make individual petals which radiate from a central point. Add a blob of yellow to the centre.

FRILLED BLIND

Blinds are the more practical option for a kitchen window, where curtains tend to get in the way of its practical function and can end up looking rather limp in the steamy, sometimes greasy atmosphere. Yet roller blinds, attractive as they are, do not always create the right kind of ambience for a country-style kitchen. The answer is a frilled blind which offers the best of both worlds, being practical yet still soft and pretty for that country cottage look. You can use any kind of fabric providing it is not too bulky, otherwise it will not gather itself into gentle flounces. Sheer or lightweight materials work best. Sometimes called festoon or Austrian blinds, the fabric can be lined.

You will need

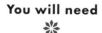

- Tape measure
- Fabric
- Needle and thread
- Scissors
- Sewing machine
- Austrian blind kit (rings, tapes, cords, cleat, screw eyes)
- Pins
- Curtain heading tape
- Curtain rail
- Wooden batten

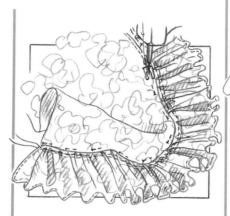

1 *Measure the window and estimate how much fabric you need: the blind can be hung inside or outside the window recess and this will affect your measurements. The length of the blind will be the hieght of the window plus 45.5cm (18in); the width will be twice that of the window. Join fabric widths if necessary, using a French seam and taking care to match any pattern. Turn under a 12mm (½in) double hem along the sides and bottom edge. To make a frill along the bottom edge, cut a 10cm (4in) strip of matching fabric, twice the fabric's width. Double hem the two short sides and one of*

the longer sides, turning each hem under about 6mm (¼in). Along the other long side, make two rows of gathering stitches and draw these up to fit the bottom edge of the blind. Put right sides together, baste and machine-stitch into position.

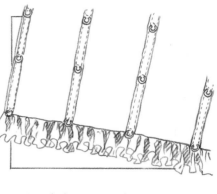

2 *Mark the position for the vertical tapes using a line of basting stitches; these should be equally spaced between 25.5 – 61cm (10 – 24in) apart. Pin and baste the tapes to these lines, starting at the lower edge and ensuring that a horizontal loop is positioned at the bottom of the blind on each length of tape. The loops should be positioned evenly across the blind so that it will gather evenly. Fold the end of each tape over 6mm (¼in) and machine-stitch into position.*

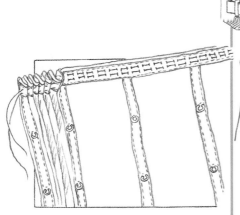

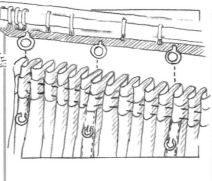

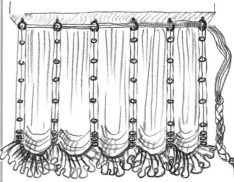

3 Fold over the top edge of the blind about 12mm (½in) and pin, baste, then machine-stitch the curtain heading tape into place. Pull the cords on the heading tape until the blind is the correct width and insert curtain hooks at 7.5cm (3in) intervals.

4 Thread the cords through the loops on the vertical tapes, starting at the opposite side of the blind from where the cleat has been fitted. Thread each cord through the relevant screw eye on the batten and knot the cords together, leaving enough loose cord for the blind to work. Do not cut off excess cord. Attach a series of eye hooks to the underside of the board, one for the top of each vertical tape.

5 Fasten the curtain rail onto a wooden batten installed at the top of the window. Fasten the cleat into position on the wall next to the blind. Hook the blind up to the curtain track, pull the cords to gather up the blind and fasten to the wall cleat.

CHAPTER SIX

ℬEDROOMS

THE LOOK OF AN ENGLISH COUNTRY-STYLE bedroom will depend on its size. Smaller cottage bedrooms generally have a lot of natural character. They often have a low or sloping ceiling, exposed beams, and maybe a tiny lead-paned or dormer window. Rooms like this need very little enhancement to reinforce that country atmosphere: a cotton rug or kelim thrown over the stripped and polished boards on the floor; a fine wooden or brass bed with plump, white broderie anglaise pillows and richly worked patchwork quilt. They need very little other furniture, except perhaps a painted chair, an old marble washstand complete with china jug and bowl, or an old chest of drawers.

COLOURS AND TEXTURES

There are two ways of tackling the decoration of a cottage bedroom: you can go for the austere look, designed especially, it seems, to complement sunlight streaming through the billowing muslin at the window and dancing on the whitewashed rough

1 *Sloping ceiling*
2 *Four poster bed*
3 *Cloth-covered bedside table*
4 *Random floral print wallpaper*
5 *Painted chest of drawers*
6 *Simple window treatment*
7 *Quilted bedcover*

Above: Stripped and polished floorboards create exactly the right feel on the floor for both simple cottage and grander bedrooms. Opposite: A pivoting brass rail has solved the problem of an awkward window in this simple cottage bedroom under the eaves.

plaster walls. Old samplers and hand-stitched homilies would look at home here. The furniture should bc stripped and polished or milk-painted in pastel shades. If the walls are not white, they could be delicately colourwashed in palest sunshine yellow or blush pink. Choose a simple stencil for additional decoration. The bedcover, as the focal point of the room, can be a celebration of some traditional hand-stitched craft such as appliqué, patchwork or quilting.

Alternatively, choose the style of a snug and cosy cottage bedroom where there are tiny flowers everywhere you look: a small-print wallpaper up and over the walls and ceiling; matching curtains at the window with frilled pelmet and tie-backs; and scatter cushions among the frills and lace on the bed. It should all be executed in shades of an English country garden – deep dusky pinks, delphinium and speedwell blues; sage green and butterscotch yellow ochre, all against a background of rich cream, so much more subtle and restful than bright white.

BEDS

For a larger bedroom you might prefer to adopt the English manor-house style where pride of place is given to the bed, ideally an elaborately carved four poster hung with heavy drapes. If this is not practical, choose a half-tester or create an improvised effect using poles or rails and an abundance of inexpensive fabric.

Hand-mixed or thinned paints will produce an authentic patchy finish for walls in country bedrooms.

FLOORS AND WALLS

To go with the bed you need stained and polished floorboards, with fine rugs or an oriental carpet. Walls can be painted, or papered with elegant stripes, a large floral design, ribbons or a trellis effect – not a small-print which loses all its impact over larger areas. The window treatment needs to be more elaborate, too, perhaps borrowing some of the ideas more usually seen in living rooms: floor-to-ceiling lined curtains, tie-backs, a pelmet, maybe a windowseat – to give the window even greater emphasis.

FURNITURE

Consider other items such as a full-length cheval mirror, a double dressing table and an ottoman at the end of the bed. Small circular occasional tables are useful and can be purchased quite cheaply and covered with a cloth (or cloths) to match other furnishing details.

PROJECTS

You will need
✳

- Hammer
- Nail punch
- Strips of wood
- Wood adhesive
- Plane
- Wood filler
- Power sander
- Protective mask
- Broom or vacuum cleaner
- Mop or cloth
- Small belt sander
- Sandpaper
- Clear polyurethane varnish
- White spirit
- Varnish brush

STRIPPED FLOORBOARDS

A stripped board floor, patiently sanded and varnished, not only looks great in country-style bedrooms and living rooms, it is also extremely hardwearing and needs very little maintenance. It makes the perfect background for rugs and dhurries but, should you want the floor to look a little more ornamental, it can be stained or bleached in a variety of colours and patterns. Alternatively, you could stencil a border around the room using paint before the final coat of varnish. The sanding process is dusty, dirty and hard work; you will have to hire a heavy-duty sanding machine from your local hire shop for such a large area. These are available by the day or weekend and you should try and assess how many floors you need to do and have them ready on the day to save hire time. Make sure the model you hire has a collection bag for the dust. It is also important before you spend a lot of time and effort to decide whether a floor is worth sanding. If the boards are too worn, are badly damaged or have been stained, it would be better to consider laying a new floor.

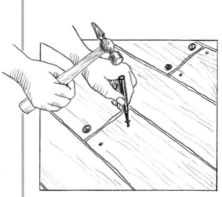

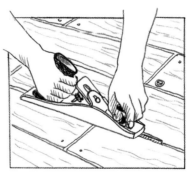

1 *Before sanding, carefully check over the floor surface to make sure there are no spiked carpet gripper strips or protruding nails and screws likely to rip the sander belt. Strips can be levered up; any nails should be knocked below the surface using a hammer and nail punch. Equally important, screws must be countersunk.*

2 *For a neat finish you may like to fill any gaps between the boards with wedge-shaped pieces of timber; these can be stained to match the rest of the floor. Spread a little wood adhesive on the wedges to keep them in place. Knock them in using a hammer and an offcut of timber to prevent damaging the wood. Plane the wood smooth to make it level with the rest of the floor. For a really fine finish, smaller cracks can be repaired using wood filler.*

continued over ➤

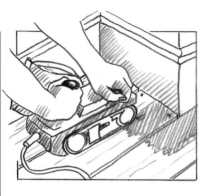

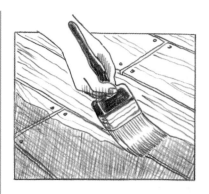

3 *When the boards are adequately prepared, fit the power sander with the coarsest sanding belt. Always wear a protective mask when using the power sander as the dust gets everywhere. Start sanding, manoevring the machine carefully – it is slow and heavy – and make sure you keep it moving or you will sand out unsightly dips and hollows. Begin by moving the machine diagonally across the boards, overlapping each journey by around 7.5cm (3in) to ensure you do not miss any areas. It will be too bulky to reach right up to the skirting boards, so you will have to stop short and finish the job later using a small belt sander. Turn off the machine as you turn to go back the other way or it will scratch the boards. When you have covered the greater part of the floor, sweep up the dust with a broom or vacuum cleaner and mop the whole floor. Fit the medium abrasive belt.*

4 *This time sand up and down the grain of the boards, overlapping your route and turning off the machine every time you turn as before. Sweep and mop away the dust then fit the fine sanding belt. Repeat the sanding process as for the medium-grade sanding. To finish, use a small belt sander to go around the edges and corners of the room, making sure you work with the grain of the wood, never against it. You may need to sand by hand to reach right into the corners. Sweep or vacuum up all the dust and finish with a damp mop. Allow to dry.*

5 *Dilute the first coat of varnish with about 10 per cent of white spirit and brush it along the grain of the wood. Apply with a suitable varnish brush, taking care that you do not spread it too thickly. Leave to dry completely. Sand lightly, dust with a soft cloth and apply two or three further undiluted coats as necessary, making sure you sand and clean between coats.*

CIRCULAR TABLECLOTH

A long circular cloth falling to the floor over an occasional table always looks great and is a wonderfully easy way to breathe life into an old piece of furniture which has seen better days, or to disguise a new foldaway chipboard model. A second, shorter cloth on top, whether circular or square, makes the effect even more impressive.

You will need

- Fabric
- Tape measure
- Needle and thread
- Scissors
- Pins
- Iron
- Tailor's chalk

- Sheet of paper
- String
- Pencil
- Drawing pin
- Lace, tassels or braid trim
- Fringing

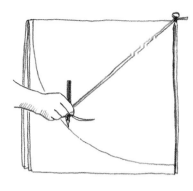

2 *Cut out a sheet of paper to the same size as the folded, that is, quartered fabric. Onto this, sketch a perfectly curved radius using a piece of string and a pencil pivoted on a central drawing pin, like an improvised pair of compasses.*

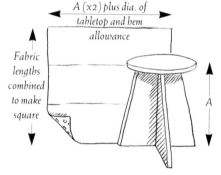

A (x2) plus dia. of tabletop and hem allowance

Fabric lengths combined to make square

A

Cut the fabric to the correct widths, making sure it is on the straight grain. Join by pinning, basting and stitching, then press the seams open so that they lie as flat as possible. Fold the fabric in four: first in half lengthwise, then widthwise. Mark the intersection of the folds with tailor's chalk.

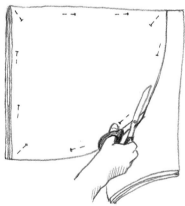

1 *Allow sufficient fabric to cut out a square with a side equal to the total diameter of the proposed tablecloth. Circular cloths almost invariably require joining to produce sufficient width and those joins should always be made by adding two new sections of identical width to a central panel to get a balanced effect. To calculate the width of your cloth, measure from the table edge to the floor (A) and double this measurement. Add this figure to the diameter of the tabletop plus 3cm (1in) for a narrow hem allowance.*

3 *Cut along this line to create a paper pattern. Lay this over the folded material, taking care to match up the central points. Pin in position and cut the fabric along the curved line. Remove the paper pattern and open up the folded fabric to reveal a perfectly circular cloth. Pin the hem, baste, hemstitch and press. The edge can, if you wish, be finished with lace, tassels or braid.*

CHAPTER SEVEN

Bathrooms

69

FOR A LONG TIME, THE MAJORITY OF ENGLISH bathrooms, let alone country ones, were completely lacking in style and charm. They were functional rooms - cold, characterless and often ignored when the home was redesigned and decorated. More recently, though, there has been a surge of interest in the design and colour of sanitary-ware, in paint and paper specially developed for use in bathrooms, and even in co-ordinating towels and accessories. One of the most important trends in this new emphasis has been a revival in the Victorian/Edwardian English look which is ideally suited to country-style homes: all-white sanitary-ware, handsome roll-top baths with their own ball and claw feet, stripped pine washstands and shiny brass accessories.

WALLS

The style can be adapted to any size and situation. If your bathroom is tiny and awkwardly shaped, it pays to panel it, incorporating built-in features such as cupboards and shelving within the space

1 *Stencilled motif*
2 *Stripped and stained floorboards*
3 *Old-fashioned cast iron bath*
4 *Varnished wooden toilet seat*

5 *White sanitary-ware*
6 *Simple colourful curtains threaded on a metal rail*
7 *Colourwashed walls*

available. Both bath and basin – and the toilet too if you wish – can be built in without losing their traditional look, particularly if you choose the right kind of sanitary-ware. This is also an excellent way to give your bathroom a new look without the expense of changing a whole suite, particularly if you buy a new toilet seat to match your chosen finish. The timber can be stained and given three or four coats of polyurethane varnish to protect it from steam and splashes. But if you feel this will look too overpowering in a small space, the most stylish treatment is to paint the panelling palest aquamarine, deep cream or a similar pastel shade. This will create a suitably light and airy impression while maximizing the room's potential for storage and washing facilities.

Should you like a little extra decoration, stencilling borders around the wall or along the side of the bath panelling is very effective and can incorporate a suitable theme such as fish, boats or shells. Bathroom paints are specially formulated to avoid condensation and problems with mould; you can make a softer and more textured look by rag-rolling or sponging one shade over another. Soft vinyl wallpapers can be perfect for country bathrooms where you want a pretty room full of florals; there are both large and small designs to choose from, and there are also matching fabrics suitable for blinds or curtains.

FURNISHINGS

Larger rooms offer even more scope for being creative; in older properties the bathroom is often sited in a converted bedroom, especially in houses where there was not one in existence before. There may be interesting architectural details visible, such as mouldings or even an open fireplace. Large rooms can afford to consider the rather grand unfitted look, complete with free-standing roll-top bath, a washstand or generously sized pedestal basin, maybe even a comfy chair or small sofa. The right choice of colours and textures is especially important in bathrooms: with the wrong shade of blue and too many hard shiny surfaces on tiles and sanitary-ware, you could create a very chilly, uncomfortable atmosphere.

*A stencilled design can be chosen to
match other decorative features
and be applied to walls and fittings
for a very relaxing and highly
attractive atmosphere.*

Even a few shells applied to a circular mirror frame makes it the perfect country bathroom accessory.

Tiles come in an infinitely wide choice of traditional shades and styles which include pictures, patterns, borders and even complete murals. In the country-style bathroom, to prevent them looking too clinical or over-powering, they are most likely to be used only as a splashback behind bath or basin, or to dado level.

Accessories such as soap dishes, towel rails and toilet roll holders can all be chosen to suit your particular scheme: pine and mahogany, glossy brass and chrome, flower-decorated or plain coloured ceramics.

WINDOWS AND FLOORS

Bathroom windows can be difficult to dress. For a country-style bathroom, you could choose small curtains held to the side with matching tie-backs; alternatively, you could have a flouncy Austrian blind which does not get in the way of other features.

On the floor, polished boards and a comfortable cotton rug or dhurrie would be suitable. In downstairs bathrooms, where there may be quarry tiles or stone flags, the soft rug is even more essential. You can achieve the same look – of stone, tiles, cork or timber – with vinyl, available in tiles or by the sheet, to produce a far warmer and more comfortable surface underfoot.

The final touch, to give that real country feel, is an attractively framed mirror, a few dried flowers, and maybe a collection of pictures and prints. The bathroom does not have to be cold and clinical and the secret is to tackle its decoration the same way you would any other room in the English country-style home.

Whether stained and varnished or painted, panelling has an extra use in the bathroom for boxing in ugly pipes and sanitary-ware.

PROJECTS

You will need
❋

- Jig saw
- Plywood
- Piece of mirror glass
- Selection of shells
- Epoxy resin adhesive
- Piece of plain glass (optional)
- Cotton wool (optional)
- Tile cement (optional)
- Tweezers (optional)
- Scalpel blade (optional)
- Varnish or nail varnish
- Artist's brush
- Fixing rings

1 *Using a jig saw, cut a piece of plywood to the correct shape of the base and around 10cm (4in) wider than the glass all around. Glue the mirror glass to the plywood. Start gluing a mass of shells onto the*

SHELL MIRROR

Shellwork was very popular with the Victorians who used masses of different shells to cover frames and boxes or to create amazingly detailed pictures, tiny figurines, and even bunches of fake flowers. A shell-framed mirror would look splendid in a country bathroom where the shell theme could be continued through shell- motif stencils, soap dishes and appliquéd towels. You could collect the shells on visits to the coast at home or abroad, or you can buy them in seaside shops or from craft suppliers. No special talent is required for shellwork, providing the shells are applied close together to produce a massed effect, but the more creative-minded might like to try their hand at making shell flowers or a symmetrical design. You can buy mirror glass in all shapes and sizes including circles and ovals from any good glass supplier. Alternatively, buy an old mirror cheaply from a junk shop and carefully remove the existing frame.

plywood frame using a quick-drying epoxy resin adhesive. Take care to cover the wood completely; the shells must overlap the edge of the glass slightly. Shells may be chosen at random providing you keep the arrangement balanced and avoid positioning the larger shells more on one side than the other. You may prefer to plan out where your shells will go before you glue them down. Always work with the frame laid down horizontally until the adhesive has dried.

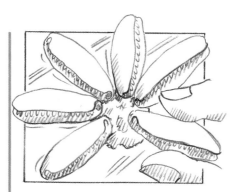

2 *The more adventurous might like to experiment with making shell flowers to add to their frame arrangement. The flowers need to be made separately and then glued*

in place when finished. You will need to work horizontally on a piece of plain glass until the flowers have dried. Using tiny matching shells as petals, all kinds of flowers can be made. Begin by soaking a small button of cotton wool in tile cement and placing on your glass. Press the shells into place – you may find tweezers useful for positioning the tiniest ones – and leave the finished flowers horizontal for the cement to dry. When dry, remove the completed flowers from the glass using a sharp scalpel blade. Then glue them to the arrangement with epoxy resin adhesive. Depending on how many you have the patience to make, the mirror could be ringed around with flowers or have just a couple as an extra decoration.

3 Finish with a thin coat of clear varnish applied with a fine artist's brush. You can also use nail varnish in suitably pink pearly shades for an attractive finish. When dry, apply fixing rings to the back of the frame (bearing in mind it will be heavy) and hang it on the wall.

STENCILLED WALL

Stencilling is a quick and effective way to add interest and colour to walls as well as to furniture and floors. It is inexpensive, too, as it uses very little paint. In a country cottage interior, it is probably best to keep to the simpler stencil motifs, maybe with a suitably rustic theme such as flowers, fruit or ears of wheat. Elaborate art deco designs and wide complicated borders employing several colours should be kept for town houses. You can buy a wide range of ready-made stencils from art shops and decorating stores, but you can easily make your own for more original effects, maybe even devised to echo other themes and patterns in the room.

75

You will need

- Tracing paper
- Pencil
- Paper
- Brown manilla paper
- Linseed oil
- Thin acetate (optional)
- Scalpel blade or craft knife
- Chalk
- Masking tape or Spraymount
- Paint
- Old plate or saucer
- Stencil brush
- Card or newspaper
- White spirit

1 To create a stencil, trace your chosen motif onto a piece of paper and then simplify it into stencil form, remembering to leave sufficient ties to link the different areas. It can easily be enlarged or reduced to the required size at your local photocopy shop. Transfer the design onto brown manilla paper brushed with linseed oil and allowed to dry to make it more durable, or onto thin acetate. Cut out the stencil using a sharp scalpel blade or craft knife, leaving a wide margin above and below.

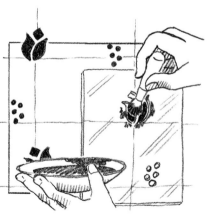

2 Chalk in guidelines on your wall to ensure that the design will be kept straight. When applying a border to walls in older houses, go by eye; never use a straight edge to achieve a straight line as the ceiling line is probably anything but level

continued over ➤

and your design will appear to slope. Keep the stencil tightly in place using masking tape or spray mount. This should ensure the colour does not leak underneath and spoil the effect. Begin painting by pouring a little paint into an old plate or saucer and dabbing a stubby stencil brush into it until loaded. Remove excess paint by pouncing the brush on card or newspaper - do this every time to maintain even colour distribution and avoid any thickening effect. Dab the brush onto the cut-out areas of the stencil, which will produce a soft, broken effect when the stencil is lifted. Put the stencil in position for the next motif.

76

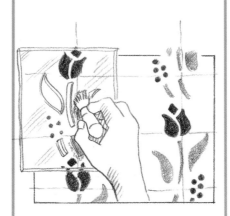

3 *To add a secondary colour you will need another stencil, which should match the original but with different areas cut out. It is useful to have some guidelines so that the stencil can be positioned correctly. When the design is complete, allow the paint to dry. Clean the stencils themselves with white spirit.*

PANELLED WALL

Panelling a room or half panelling a wall is a fine way to disguise poor plaster or create a different effect: and how you treat those boards will define the finished atmosphere. Stained and varnished, they can seem quite grand in an old-fashioned way and will make any room feel cosier. When painted – particularly in pastel blues, lemon or white – they have a much simpler, cottage effect and will even appear to lighten a room. The boards are quite simple to fit and offer an easy-to-maintain, durable alternative to paint or paper. Traditionally, the boards are fixed to battens with pins but there are also new clip systems which can offer invisible fixing.

You will need
❋

- Tongue-and-groove panelling
- Silicone water-repellant
- Battens
- Hammer
- Masonry nails
- Spirit level
- Hardboard (optional)
- Pins or clips
- Nail punch

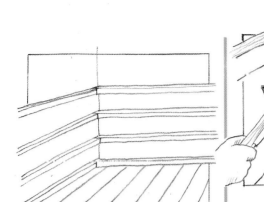

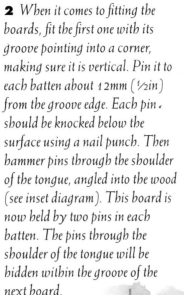

1 *Bring the timber into the room where it is going to be fitted at least a week beforehand. This allows its moisture content to adjust to that of the room. Should you bring the boards from outside into a centrally heated room, for example, the timber will shrink and, if fitted too soon, will create ugly gaps in between boards. To prepare a wall for panelling, check that it is not damp. Treating the wall with a silicone water repellant before the panelling goes up will prevent water coming in on an outside wall. You will need to remove any skirting boards and picture rails to facilitate fitting the supportive battens. Fit the battens at approximately 40cm (16in) intervals, using a spirit level to make sure they are straight. You might need to pack them behind with pieces of hardboard if the walls are uneven. Fix the battens to the wall with masonry nails.*

2 *When it comes to fitting the boards, fit the first one with its groove pointing into a corner, making sure it is vertical. Pin it to each batten about 12mm (½in) from the groove edge. Each pin should be knocked below the surface using a nail punch. Then hammer pins through the shoulder of the tongue, angled into the wood (see inset diagram). This board is now held by two pins in each batten. The pins through the shoulder of the tongue will be hidden within the groove of the next board.*

3 *Subsequent boards only need one pin in each batten, hammered into the shoulder of the tongue. The interlocking nature of the tongues and grooves will keep the panelling in place. When you have finished, fill in the holes made by the nail punch in the first board with matching wood filler. Clip systems vary and you should follow manufacturer's instructions.*

CHAPTER EIGHT

Studies and Libraries

FEW HOUSES ARE LUCKY ENOUGH TO HAVE room for a personal library or even a separate study but, with more and more people moving out to the country to work from home, an office or study area is becoming more of a priority. It need not be a room in its own right but may be fitted into an existing area of the house, such as the hall or on the landing, or even in a corner of the kitchen. Alternatively, it can be combined with another room such as a spare bedroom, hobby or family room. Modern electrical equipment such as television, computer, fax and phone can always be hidden away inside specially fitted cupboards and drawers, with swivel-out facilities if necessary.

WALLS

Even if it is to be only in a small corner of the house or a dual-purpose room, you will want to reproduce the atmosphere of the country house library or den: a room to retreat to on long wet afternoons with a good book, or somewhere you can concentrate on

1 *Panelled walls*	**4** *Comfortable chair*
2 *Plenty of shelving*	**5** *Reading lamp*
3 *Large desk*	**6** *Richly coloured fabric*

Panelled walls and an open fire evoke that gentleman's club atmosphere. Make the most of any alcoves and recesses to fit extra shelving.

paperwork without the distractions of everyday life. Timber panelling on the walls, a dark, detailed, heavy wallpaper with a striped, paisley or similarly masculine design and even fabric such as coloured felt stretched across battens, are traditional treatments. Framed prints add to the atmosphere. Make a collection of your favourite subjects, whether it be hunting prints, Victorian newspaper cartoons, fashion plates or old maps. Ideally, your chosen pictures should be given matching frames and hung close together on the wall to create most impact. Larger paintings – maybe of local views or countryside scenes – in heavy, ornate gilt frames can be highlighted with special overhead spotlights.

FURNITURE
Essential furniture includes the desk, preferably old and large, made of oak, yew, pine or mahogany, and with plenty of shelves, drawers and compartments. To sit at it comfortably, choose either the

traditional captain's chair with wide wooden arms to lean on or a padded leather swivel seat. For long reading sessions, or for relaxing with a pipe or a box of chocolates, a leather or velvet easy chair, high backed to keep out the draughts and wide enough to curl up in, is the ideal, perhaps with matching footstool.

Lighting should be concentrated on the easy chair or desk area to make reading and working easier; concealed spotlights or flexible lamps are the best option here. Built-in shelving or free-standing library bookshelves are useful not only for books but for the

This antiqued desk fits perfectly at the end of the bed in a grandly furnished country bedroom. It has been hand-finished in witty imitation of old-fashioned haberdasher's drawers, restyled to suit its bedroom setting.

If you are lucky enough to have a fine antique desk like this one, it sets the tone for the room immediately.

occasional ornament and favourite object too. When planning shelving it is a good idea to allow extra shelf space for your book collection to grow over the years.

The look and general atmosphere might be created anywhere in the country-style home but, if you are lucky enough to have a whole room you can devote to the theme, an open fire for winter afternoons completes the scheme – relaxing by a radiator would not be the same at all! It may be worth considering a gas flame-effect fire rather than coal or logs if the room is to be used infrequently as it is quicker and easier to use.

$\mathcal{P}$ROJECTS

FRAMING A PICTURE

Framing your own pictures and prints is far less expensive than having it done professionally and will encourage you to have more of them on the walls. A massed arrangement of frames on a wall can be tremendously effective as a decorative feature, especially if the frames are all matching or the pictures are linked by a country theme. Look out for inexpensive frames at auction sales and in junk shops: you can always replace the existing picture with one of your own if you do not like it or it is damaged. Doing your own framing also offers an excellent opportunity to frame all manner of material which has pictorial potential, from pictures cut out from glossy magazines to family photographs, local maps, or colour plates taken from damaged antique books.

You will need

- Picture
- Steel rule
- Stout coloured card
- Craft knife
- Adhesive tape
- Picture frame
- 2mm picture glass
- Methylated spirit
- Lint-free cloth
- Backing board
- Glazing sprigs
- Pin hammer
- Masking tape
- Screw eyes or picture rings
- Picture wire

1 *Most material for display benefits from being set in a cardboard mount larger than itself, which acts like a window and focuses attention on the artwork. It also serves to hold it away from the glass. Mounting card is available in a wide range of colours, textures and thicknesses. Measure the picture and cut an opening or 'window' in the card about 6mm (¼in) smaller than the picture with allowance for a wider margin at the bottom. Use a sharp knife and steel rule, cutting as cleanly as possible with no nicks. Lay the picture on a table or level work surface, slightly overlapping the edge. Lay the cut mount over the*

picture and keep it in place at the bottom of the mount with a small piece of adhesive tape on the back of the picture. Now turn them over and tape the top edge of the picture to the mount.

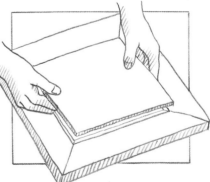

2 *Assemble everything you need on a level surface cleaned of any dust and grease. Lay the frame face downwards, clean the glass on both sides with methylated spirit and a lint-free cloth, and fit it gently into the rebate of the frame. Then lower the mounted picture and backing board into the frame, making sure that the picture is centred.*

continued over ➤

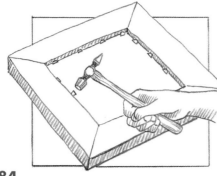

3 *Press glazing sprigs at regular intervals against the backing board and tap them into position in the inner edge of the frame with a small pin hammer.*

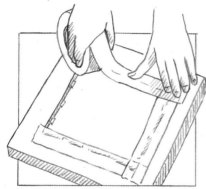

4 *Seal the join between the frame and the backing board from dust and dirt with a strip of masking tape. The tape will also protect the wall (and other pictures if they are stacked before hanging) from being scratched by the sprigs.*

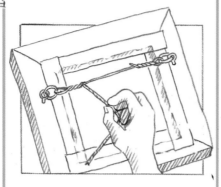

5 *To finish, screw a couple of screw eyes or picture rings directly into the frame about 10 – 15cm (4 – 6in) from the top; thread through a piece of picture wire and twist it to secure. Then hang the picture.*

ANTIQUED FURNITURE

Genuine antiques are expensive, especially if you are looking to buy large items of furniture such as a desk, a table or cupboard. Yet a few old pieces, full of character and quietly displaying the scars of many years' wear and tear, are an essential element of the English country home: stylish but comfortable and a little careworn. Even reproduction furniture, although often faithful in every detail, does not have that well-used feel to it. That said, it is possible to take a brand-new, whitewood piece of wooden furniture and, providing the style is suitable and it is reasonably well made, create an authentically antique appearance.

You will need
❋

- Coloured woodstain
- Housepainter's brush
- Wire wool
- Round-headed hammer
- Bunch of keys
- Nails
- Soft cloth
- Fuller's earth
- Raw umber oil colour
- Beeswax polish
- Old cotton rag
- Furniture paint or varnish stripper

1 Begin by staining the wood a suitably mellow shade of whichever timber you wish it to resemble: dark brown for aged oak, for example, or a dark honeyed gold to represent antique pine. If the item already has a paint or varnish finish this will have to be removed first by using a proprietary stripper. This will have an instant ageing effect.

2 Round off any corners and soften the edges of the piece by rubbing with wire wool and blunting with a round-headed hammer. You can dint, scratch and scar other surfaces by beating with a bunch of keys and bashing with a hammer. Woodworm holes can even be reproduced using a hammer and nail.

3 When you have knocked all the newness out of it and generally mellowed the piece, you can artificially add the grime of centuries. Using a soft cloth, rub fuller's earth and raw umber oil colour into the dints and scratches, into corners and along the edges where dirt tends to collect. Apply a couple of treatments of beeswax polish with a dirty duster to finish.

CHAPTER NINE

CHILDREN'S ROOMS

CHILDREN'S ROOMS ARE NOTORIOUSLY DIFFICULT to furnish and this is no less true in a country-style home with its awkwardly shaped rooms and often limited dimensions. The problem here is most frequently solved by turning to the traditional nursery for inspiration, where old-fashioned design ideas backed up by modern solutions to requirements such as safety and storage can be a most satisfactory combination. Even older children can find it great fun to go back in time with traditional furnishings such as four-poster beds, or to find their room converted into a fairytale castle or an enchanted forest with a little clever application of paint or paper.

In houses lucky enough to boast a useful attic space, this is often commandeered for the children's use, especially where the children may be older and can be trusted to play or sleep in their own 'den'. Effectively removed from the main part of the house, the inevitable mess and noise can be contained, which relieves a lot of pressure from the rest of the household. The attic may be used as a playroom or hobby room, or be divided into bedrooms, perhaps

1 Stripped pine bed
2 Patchwork quilt
3 Practical easy-clean flooring
4 Fun features
5 Plenty of storage
6 Traditional nursery toys
7 Brightly painted motifs

Even if you are not confident of your artistic abilities, découpage can be used to apply pictures and motifs to any clear, dry surface.

using furniture or storage units as flexible room dividers. This is the perfect place to provide room for large play/hobby activities such as a model village or toy train set. In a home where space is limited, it is often well worth the investment of a loft conversion where the attic is not instantly habitable. Important require-ments are safe and easy access via stairs or steps and some form of lighting and venti-lation. Special windows are easily installed into the roof area, providing they do not contravene any planning restrictions relevant to your particular property.

FLOORS

The basic elements of country style – the simply painted walls and the use of natural, sturdy materials – make an excellent background for furnishing a child's room in traditional style. On the floor, you need something that is warm yet practical to clean, so polished floorboards are probably not the best choice, particularly from the point of view of noise. Choose instead a surface such as vinyl which comes in a range of fake, traditionally rustic designs such as tiles or stone flags (offering excellent play possibilities too), or cork tiles which are easily fitted and also come in a range of colours and designs. Nursery rugs provide further softness and warmth if required. To this you can add scaled-down prints such as florals or both modern cartoons and characters and old favourites specially designed for younger folk. These are available on every conceivable surface from wallpaper and curtains to lampshades, blinds, bed linen and furniture, or you could paint or appliqué your own. Colour schemes tend to be either baby pastels or bright primary shades, both of which can look good against natural surfaces such as wood and plain white walls.

FURNITURE

You can buy a wide range of scaled-down furniture and, if a child-sized four-poster or a bed and cupboards complex designed to look like a castle, seems an extravagance, you could always indulge yourself in a nursery table and matching chairs, a *trompe-l'oeil* painted toy cupboard or a stencilled toy-box. For tiny babies there are cribs and cots, changing units, and even old-fashioned nursing chairs, although an old rocking chair is a good substitute. An old-fashioned rocking horse, a doll's house or train set provide hours of enjoyable play for older children as well as reinforcing a traditional furnishing theme.

STORAGE

The secret to success when dealing with awkward shapes, such as sloping ceilings, is to build in any necessary storage facilities. Either use components which you buy and install yourself – a wide range of frames, doors, racks, drawers and hangers can be obtained – or employ a fitted-bedroom company to handle the whole job. The built-in units can be painted or papered to match the rest of the room, thus rendering awkward shapes virtually invisible, or be treated to some kind of *trompe-l'oeil* decoration to make a fun feature and interesting focal point. Other ways you can make space include

The quilt-like duvet and cot bumper have been matched to simple gingham curtains and a colourful wall frieze in this country-style nursery bedroom.

Little girls love the country cottage look with its wooden or ornate brass bed, pretty floral curtains and a luxurious mass of pillows and frills.

blocking up an existing fireplace or an awkwardly placed door to release more wall area.

SAFETY

Decorating the children's room can be fun, giving you the chance to exercise your imagination and be a little more adventurous than elsewhere in the house, but safety and practicality are of utmost importance. For example, low windows may add character to a room but they are easy to fall against or for little fingers to open; you will need to fit toughened glass and bars or safety locks. Check that electrical wiring, especially in older properties, is safe; child-proof plugs are essential and any electrical fittings or appliances should be out of reach. The old nursery open fire, even with its large safety guard, is better rejected for a wall-mounted heater or radiators; instead convert the fireplace into bookshelves or a novel dolls' house. Also, remember if using old pieces of furniture in a child's room to make sure the paint or finish is non-toxic; you can buy special lead-free nursery paints if restoring items yourself.

$\mathscr{P}$ROJECTS

You will need
❋

- Toybox
- Damp cloth
- Polyurethane varnish
- Emulsion paint
- Housepainter's brush
- Sealer
- Sandpaper
- Sharp scissors or craft knife
- Pictures to cut out
- Paper glue
- Artist's brush
- Tweezers (optional)
- Paint roller

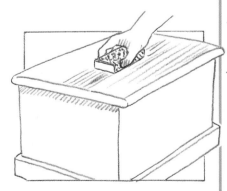

1 *Begin by preparing the surface of the toybox. Ideally, it should be as smooth as possible with no holes or cracks, and completely cleaned of grease, dirt and dust so that the paper will stick closely to it. Apply*

DÉCOUPAGED TOYBOX

Découpage is simply the art of applying cut-out pictures to any clean, dry surface, although it is most usually seen decorating furniture. It is an excellent technique for those who are not confident enough of their artistic skills to tackle a painted picture and is the ideal way to decorate a wooden toybox, chest of drawers or cupboard in the children's room with a favourite cartoon figure or nursery character. Pictures can be cut from magazines, greetings cards, catalogues and books, providing the paper is not so thin that the glue and varnish will make the picture on the reverse show through. You can buy books of old-fashioned découpage pictures from art shops; alternatively, look out for books and packets of assorted children's characters and motifs which make excellent subjects for découpage.

a coat of varnish or paint to the box, according to the finish you want. When dry, apply a coat of sealer. When this is completely dry, sand it lightly.

2 *Cut out your chosen pictures as carefully as possible with a pair of sharp scissors or a craft knife. Tilt the paper upwards slightly as you cut to help scissors around difficult details.*

3 *Apply the paper glue to the reverse of the pictures using a small artist's brush to make sure it is only thinly spread and reaches awkward corners. Stick the pictures onto the furniture, using tweezers if necessary to position them correctly and to avoid over-handling. Again, a small artist's brush is useful for pressing down finer details. Remove any excess glue immediately with a damp cloth.*

continued over ➤

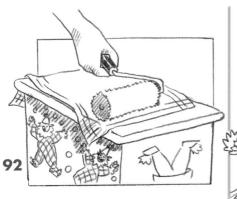

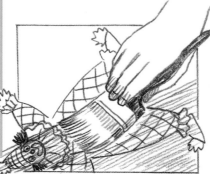

4 *Cover each side of the box in turn with a damp cloth and press over it gently with a paint roller to ensure that the pictures are well stuck down.*

5 *Leave the découpage to dry out completely before varnishing. Apply up to six coats of varnish, allowing 24 hours and a gentle rub-down with sandpaper between each coat.*

APPLIQUÉD MOTIF

Appliqué is a lovely way to decorate duvet covers, curtains, cloths, and even towels with matching motifs, especially in the nursery or children's room. A particular shape or character could be matched to a similar stencilled or painted figure on wall, cot or cupboard. There are various ways the motif can be applied depending on what it is and where it is to be used; a machine-sewed appliqué is the best option for an item that will be given hard wear. It is important that the fabric you choose for the appliqué is the same weight and type as the main fabric or it will pucker and pull. Most types of material can be used providing they are not prone to fraying easily.

You will need
❋

- Thick paper for template
- Appliqué fabric
- Sharp dressmaking scissors
- Needle and thread
- Iron
- Pins
- Tracing paper (optional)
- Sewing machine (optional)

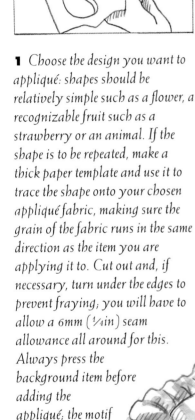

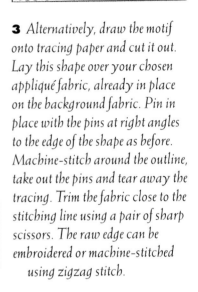

1 *Choose the design you want to appliqué: shapes should be relatively simple such as a flower, a recognizable fruit such as a strawberry or an animal. If the shape is to be repeated, make a thick paper template and use it to trace the shape onto your chosen appliqué fabric, making sure the grain of the fabric runs in the same direction as the item you are applying it to. Cut out and, if necessary, turn under the edges to prevent fraying; you will have to allow a 6mm (¼in) seam allowance all around for this. Always press the background item before adding the appliqué; the motif itself should only be pressed if you want a crisp, flattened appearance rather than a raised one.*

2 *Pin your shape onto the background fabric, placing the pins at right angles to the edges of the appliqué, never around the edge. Stab stitch all around as invisibly as you can using matching thread and a fine needle. Use cotton or silk thread for natural fabrics and synthetic thread for synthetic fabric. The edge can be embroidered over if desired.*

3 *Alternatively, draw the motif onto tracing paper and cut it out. Lay this shape over your chosen appliqué fabric, already in place on the background fabric. Pin in place with the pins at right angles to the edge of the shape as before. Machine-stitch around the outline, take out the pins and tear away the tracing. Trim the fabric close to the stitching line using a pair of sharp scissors. The raw edge can be embroidered or machine-stitched using zigzag stitch.*

$\mathcal{I}$NDEX

95

ACKNOWLEDGEMENTS

Photographs courtesy of:
Richard Bryant/Arcaid p. 82; Richard Bryant/Arcaid/The Mount Vernon
Ladies' Association of the Union p. 62; Richard Bryant/Arcaid/Susie Jenkin
p. 38; Ken Kirkwood/Arcaid pp. 5, 28–9, 31, 60–61, 81; Lucinda
Lambton/Arcaid pp. 36–7, 63; Camera Press/Appeltofft p. 41; Henrietta
from the Capri range by Crown Wallcoverings: 01254 704213 p. 54;
Dragons of Walton Street Ltd: 0171 589 3795 p. 88; from the Naturals
Collection by Dulux: 01753 550555 p. 90; Fired Earth: 01295 812088 pp. 5,
40, 78–9; Tim Beddow/Homes & Gardens/Robert Harding Syndication p.
21; Simon Brown/Country Homes & Interiors/Robert Harding Syndication
pp. 17, 64; Andreas von Einsiedel/Country Homes & Interiors/Robert
Harding Syndication pp. 4, 25; Brian Harrison/Perfect Home/Robert
Harding Syndication pp. 68–9; Brian Harrison/Period Living/Robert
Harding Syndication pp. 10, 50; Steve Lovi/Homes & Gardens/Robert
Harding Syndication p. 13; Nadia Mackenzie/Homes & Gardens/Robert
Harding Syndication pp. 48–9, 52; Fritz von der Schulenburg/Country
Homes & Interiors/Robert Harding Syndication p. 51; Polly
Wreford/Country Homes & Interiors/Robert Harding Syndication p. 72;
Chelsea pole from Harrison Drape with FADS fabric: 0121 766 6111 p. 32;
Hayloft Woodwork: 0181 747 3510 pp. 86–7; Houses & Interiors pp. 14,
24; Mothercare UK Ltd: 01923 241000 pp. 5, 89; The Stencil Store: 01923
285577 pp. 42, 71; Sunway Blinds p. 39; Renaissance towels by Christy:
0161 954 9322 p. 73; Warner Fabrics: 01908 366900 p. 7; Wicanders floor
covering: 01403 710001 pp. 22–3; Woodstock Furniture Ltd: 0171 245
9989 pp. 53, 80.